MW00861618

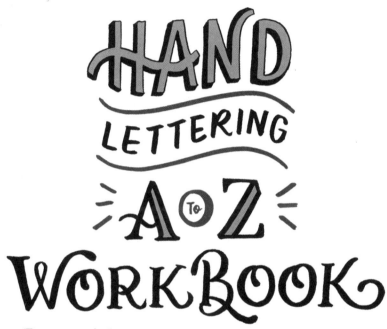

HAND LETTERING A to Z WORKBOOK

Essential Instruction and 80+ Worksheets for Modern and Classic Styles

Abbey Sy

ROCKPORT

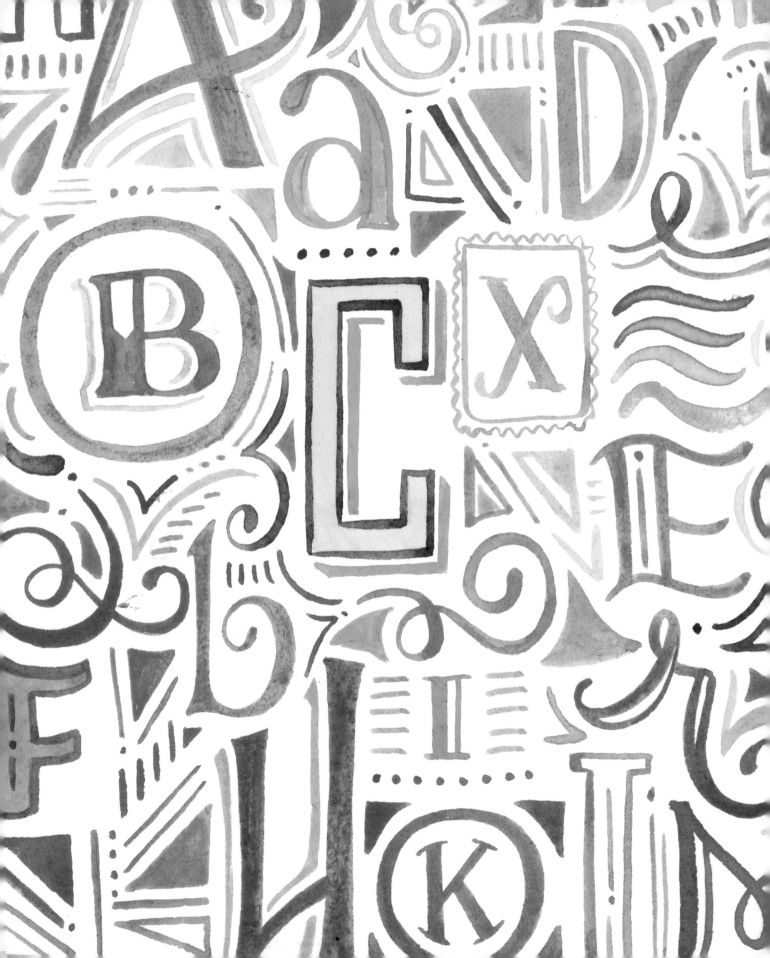

Contents

Introduction

We've seen it everywhere, undeniable evidence of the analog in our digital age: From personalized greeting cards, to wall art, to large-scale sign painting work, hand lettering has become a way for creative self-expression to shine through. And as a hand lettering artist myself, finding ways to make this art form more accessible to everyone is one of my life missions.

A follow-up to my first two books on the subject—*Hand Lettering A to Z* and *The Complete Photo Guide to Hand Lettering and Calligraphy*—*Hand Lettering A to Z Workbook* was created with lettering enthusiasts in mind, whether they're just starting out or are honing their hand lettering skills.

In addition to hand lettering basics, this book includes perforated practice sheets featuring a variety of font styles, to build your skills and to use as reference for creating your own letterforms. There are also practice sheets for embellishments and flourishes for enhancing your work, and quotes for exploring lettering layouts. The rules and grids on the practice sheets are there to guide you, but feel free to write, draw, and doodle on them, both front and back.

How To Use This Book

Hand Lettering A to Z Workbook is designed to track your progress developing your hand lettering skills. Here's how to use it.

1. **READ UP!** We've included hand lettering information and how-tos to help jumpstart (or refresh) your knowledge. These can be found at the beginning of this book; you can always go back to them if you need to review some tips and techniques.

2. **USE THE PRACTICE PAGES.** Each worksheet is designed for you to practice your skills on, so it's best to kickstart using this book by filling those up. Depending on which font style/s you're working on, you can do the worksheets in order (from the first page to the last), or vice-versa.

3. **TAKE NOTES.** After filling your worksheets with strokes and letters, revisit them to see which areas you would like to improve. Do you need to dedicate more practice time to specific strokes? Do you want to try other pens to see which works best? These self-evaluations are an important part of advancing your skills.

4. **ENJOY THE JOURNEY!** Don't pressure yourself too much. Practice at your own convenience—whether every day or twice a week, embrace your pace, keeping in mind that nothing amazing happens overnight.

May this workbook inspire and guide you on your journey to becoming a hand lettering artist, and the reminder to enjoy it remain with you.

Always be creating,

Abbey

Essential Terminology

This section offers a quick summary of some important lettering terms.

TYPOGRAPHY is the art of putting together various typefaces in order to create a work of art. The earliest form was blackletter, the first-ever typeface developed by Johannes Gutenberg, the inventor of the movable-type printing press.

CALLIGRAPHY—the art of writing letters based on handwriting—involves the correct formation of characters, the ordering of letter parts, and the harmony of proportions. Traditional calligraphy, which is rendered using a pointed pen with different nib types, as well as fountain pens and parallel pens, includes Spencerian, classical, roman, and italic. Recently it has modernized into brush lettering and other similar forms.

HAND LETTERING is the art of drawing letters based on draftsmanship using a variety of tools, such as pens, pencils, markers, brush pens, and others to create an illustrated medium.

This book presents warm-ups and practice sheets for three categories of lettering: sans serif, serif, and script. See examples below and pages 6 and 7 for more details.

The Language of Lettering

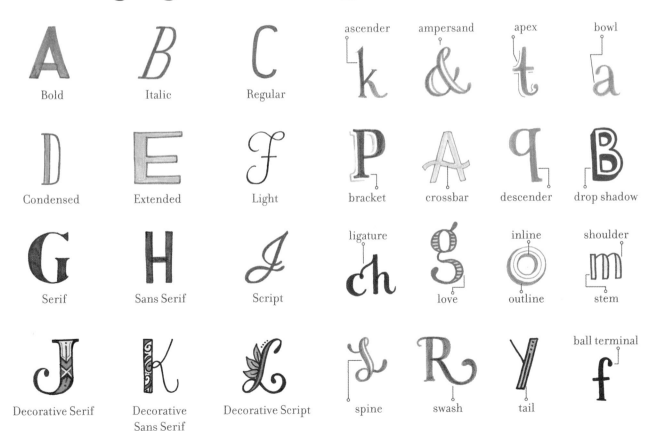

Bold	Italic	Regular
Condensed	Extended	Light
Serif	Sans Serif	Script
Decorative Serif	Decorative Sans Serif	Decorative Script

ascender, ampersand, apex, bowl
bracket, crossbar, descender, drop shadow
ligature, love, inline, outline, shoulder, stem
spine, swash, tail, ball terminal

Fonts & Type Styles

AlphaBet

Each alphabet that you design is a font: a set of characters with a specific style and size. The term *font* is often used interchangeably with *type style* when it comes to printing.

In hand lettering as well as printing, there are three main categories of fonts—sans serif, serif, and script—which are the type styles featured in the practice sheets.

SanS SERIF

A sans serif style is a font without the serifs (*sans* means "without" in French). Sans serif fonts suggest a youthful and playful approach and are often used in modern design and bold headlines. Most websites, for example, use sans serif fonts frequently as the text and headlines. With their streamlined, uncluttered, modern look, sans serif fonts are great starting points for creative modifications.

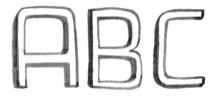

ABC

Example 1: Grotesque *(modern)*

ABC

Example 2: Square *(definite end with fewer curves)*

ABC

Example 3: Geometric *(inspired by geometric shapes)*

SERIF

A serif font style has short lines at the ends of letter strokes. Thumb through an old book, magazine, or any printed material and you'll likely notice that most of it was printed with a serif font. This style exudes a classic and traditional feel when it's used in hand lettering. But although it's classic, you can easily have fun with it. Add a little extra length to a serif and it could start to suggest a vine or a spider's web or a spool of thread that might become the creative spark for an entirely new creative font.

Script

Script lettering flows much like our own handwriting. Also known as cursive, it's a loose font style that allows you to join letters as you write. You can design script fonts in both classic and modern styles. Script is a great choice for romantic messages if you want to add flowers and flourishes. In its more modern styles, script has a lively energy that can also expand to graffiti art, retro-style script, and much more.

ABC

Example 1: Old Style *(bracketed)*

ABC

Example 2: Slab Serif *(no bracketing, low contrast)*

ABC

Example 3: Neoclassical/Didone *(single monoline)*

ABC

Example 1: Blackletter *(manuscript style dating from before the invention of movable type)*

ABC

Example 2: Calligraphic *(traditional, formal)*

ABC

Example 3: Casual *(modern)*

Tools & Materials

The Basics

Whether you have a dedicated work space where you can keep your tools and materials at hand or you work at your kitchen table, here are the basics of what you'll need.

Make sure your work surface is clean and completely smooth. If there are uneven areas on your desk or tabletop, place a sheet of mat board or thick, smooth paper under your drawing paper.

Allot ample space on your desk to work at ease. Be sure there is plenty of room to move your arms and elbows freely. If your arms feel cramped, it will be difficult to let your lettering flow.

Have a good light source. During the day, maximize your natural light source—the best light for working with color. At night, a flexible or swing-arm desk lamp is a good choice.

Always keep these tools on hand:

RULER. For measuring and creating guidelines.

BINDER CLIPS. For holding your drawing paper in place.

SOFT ERASER. For pencil marks.

PENCIL SHARPENER. A manual one is fine.

DRAWING COMPASS. For circles and curves.

Paper

Your decision to work with markers, pens, pencils, etc., will determine the type of paper you use. If you do a lot of lettering or like to doodle ideas, here are some paper types that will get you through most of your experiments. The more you letter, the more you'll find you have personal favorites.

BRISTOL PAPER. Bristol paper is smooth and reasonably heavy, so it can be used on both sides. It's perfect for pen and ink, markers, and colored pencils.

WATERCOLOR PAPER. Watercolor paper isn't just for watercolor paints—you can use it for lettering with drawing mediums too. It comes in pads or blocks and is available in three types: hot-pressed (smooth), cold-pressed (textured), and rough. Working on smooth paper is easiest for beginners. Experiment and find your favorites.

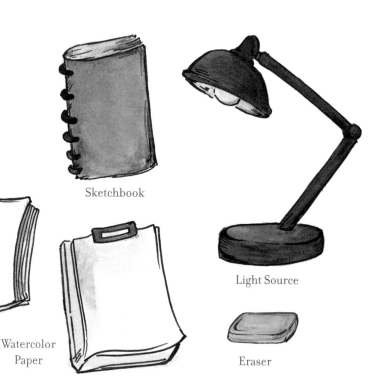

Sharpener

Drafting Paper

Sketchbook

Compass

Clips

Watercolor Paper

Light Source

Eraser

SKETCHBOOKS. Keep a sketchbook handy for working out your drafts and initial sketches. Sketchbooks are the place to practice and hone your lettering skills. I'm constantly sketching, and I've found that my best ideas for designs and layouts come from my own sketchbook.

Since I like to keep a sketchbook handy wherever I am, I find the best size for me is one that's just a little larger than the palm of my hand. Dotted or graphed sketchbooks are great for rough drafts and ideas because the grids make the measurement of letterforms easy.

SPECIALTY PAPER. Cardstock comes in different colors, finishes, textures, weights, and sizes. It's used mainly for specialized works such as gifts, souvenirs, and invitations. These papers are of superior quality and can be expensive, so they're best saved for special occasions.

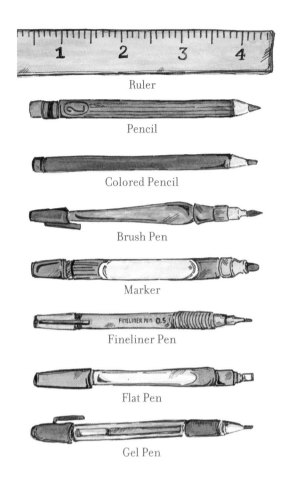

Ruler

Pencil

Colored Pencil

Brush Pen

Marker

Fineliner Pen

Flat Pen

Gel Pen

Pens & Pencils

ROUND-TIP FINELINER PEN. A fineliner pen is your best friend. Doodling and drawing with one is a lot like working with a pencil, making it the universal drawing pen for hand lettering. Fineliners are available with a variety of line weights from 0.01 to 0.8 mm. Try to have pens with at least three different weights on hand so you can play around with shadows, lines, and details in your work. My go-to weights are 0.1, 0.5, and 0.8 mm for varied thick and thin lines and details.

GEL PEN. Gel pens have a rounded tip similar to fineliners, but the writing texture is different. They are a handy choice for lettering because they are inexpensive, available everywhere, and great for rough doodling and drawing.

FLAT-TIP PEN/MARKER. Flat-tip pens have a blunt, squared nib, allowing you to make thick and thin lines as you write. They're used most often for italic and gothic lettering styles, as well as for script, with nibs available in many widths.

BRUSH PEN/MARKER. Brush-tip pens and markers are perfect for the smooth, free-flowing look of Asian calligraphy. Their flexibility makes them a good tool for gradient-heavy artworks. Brush pens come in natural or synthetic hair. Felt hair is best for beginners as it's similar to a marker's tip.

PENCIL. It's important to choose a pencil hardness that suits your personal preference. I like to keep an HB or 2H pencil on hand for sketching. These leave a relatively light mark that is easy to erase once a design has been inked. A mechanical pencil is also a good option.

COLORED PENCILS. Colored pencils are a good choice for beginners. They produce rich, vibrant colors and give a nice, organic look to your strokes. Virtually any type of paper is suitable for working with colored pencils.

Starting with Pencil

When you're just starting out, it can be helpful to "draft" letters in pencil. From there you can refine them further, then either finish them with or add color using other mediums.

   This technique can also be used to transform simple letters into dimensional letterforms to which you can add color, patterns, illustrations, or all three.

Start with Pencil, Add Colored Pencil

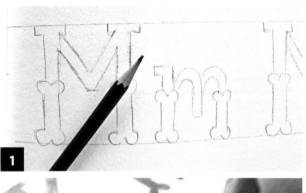

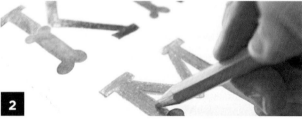

1. This process is very simple: Using a light pencil, draw your letters from A to Z, both upper- and lowercase. In the style shown, which I call "Bone Type," the somewhat blocky letters are half serif and half bone shape, so some letters have more than one bone.

2. Once you've refined the outlines, use colored pencils to fill in the areas as desired. Be sure to cover any visible pencil marks, or gently erase them as you fill in the shapes. I chose bright, contrasting colors to match this letterform's playful style.

Start with Pencil, Add Marker

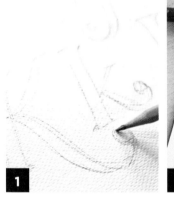

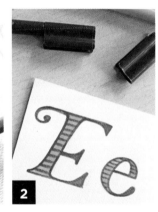

1. When you've finalized your pencil sketches, transfer them to watercolor paper. I used hot-pressed paper for this alphabet because it has a smooth texture. Lightly pencil in the letters; in this case, I left plenty of room for the exaggerated swashes of this style.

2. It's time to add color. Here, I used a round felt-tip marker to fill in the letters, then outlined them and added a striped pattern in a darker shade. Let the marker dry before erasing any visible pencil marks.

Start with Pencil, Add Fineliner

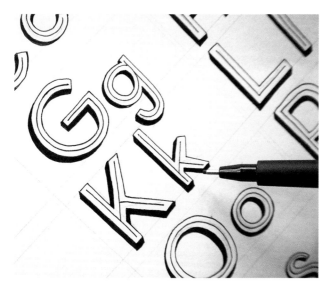

Here I created a simple inline alphabet, starting with a very basic sans serif style that I then outlined with block letterforms. I also created a shadow by thickening the left side of each letter. Using a thin fineliner pen, I traced the inline strokes I sketched with a pencil. Then, using a thick fineliner pen, I traced the block letter outlines. If desired, color and/or other patterns can be added to the interiors of the letters.

Creating Illustrations within Letterforms

Basic letters are naturally plain; through decorative lettering, they become more visually appealing. The open areas of each letter are places to get creative and add illustrations to enhance the artwork. Here are some samples for you to try.

Lined pattern (basic linear shapes and patterns)

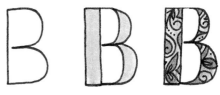

Elemental pattern (complex, connected patterns)

Embellished (botanical accent on a certain area of the letter)

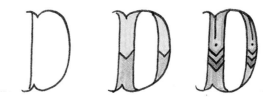

50/50 (two different patterns on both sides of the letterform)

3D style (retro effect created by adding inlines and exaggerated shadows)

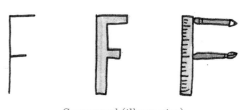

Conceptual (illustrative)

Working Freehand

Once you've gained a little lettering experience, you can try working freehand with your fineline markers and brush pens.

Script with Brush Pens

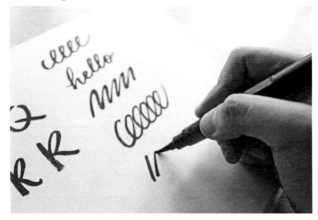

Before starting on a script font, warm up by making random strokes with a brush pen. This will help you decide how you want to grip your pen as you work. Brush pens, which come in various sizes and types, are best for script styles because they produce fluid strokes. The trick is to keep the pressure varied—light pressure to produce a thin stroke and heavy pressure to produce a thick stroke. The strokes shown here were made with an ink-based brush pen.

Creating a Hand-Lettered Layout with Markers

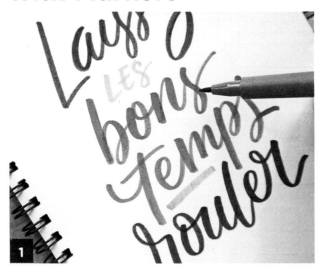

Hand-lettered quotes make great additions to the pages of your journal as well as great art pieces. Experiment with various layouts to find out how you want your journal page to look. My default placement is putting the quote in the center of the page to make room for other elements I can add later.

In the example shown here I worked directly with markers, but if you like, you can lightly pencil in your quote for guidance, then gently erase it after tracing over it with a brush pen.

1. Choose a quote you'd like to hand letter. I chose the quote "Laissez les bons temps rouler," a French quote that translates to "Let the good times roll" in English. Here I used a brush pen to letter it.

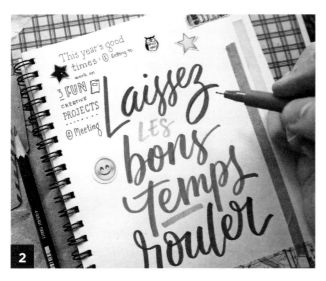

2. When you've finished, you can fill up the extra spaces with tape, stickers, or whatever other elements you'd like to add. On my page, I added stickers and tape strips first, then filled up the extra spaces with hand-lettered words and doodles with a thin fineliner pen.

Adding Bounce

In school, we were taught to practice handwriting within the lines on our practice sheets, but since hand lettering is all about drawing letters, we can tweak the structures and adjust the letters to our liking, creating our own flow based on the letters within each word. We can opt to disregard the guidelines and integrate the movement of each character into the design of each word.

Changing the heights or reducing the sizes of letters in a word makes it easier to build the composition of a quote. There are certain letters, as well, that have qualities suitable for what is called *bounce lettering*. Some letters have distinct characteristics that lend themselves to the bounce effect.

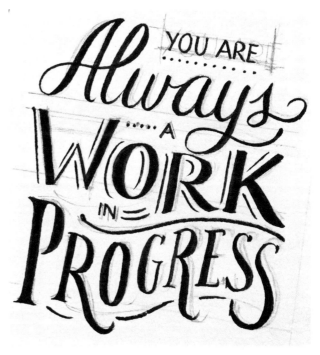

Bounced words are often lettered in script, but they don't have to be. Here's a quote in which two key words—"work" and "progress," each lettered in a different serif style—are bounced for emphasis.

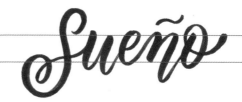

Spanish: Dream
In this example, the capital *S* and the descender on the lowercase *n* extend far below the baseline, while the ending stroke on the lowercase *o* swoops up for a final flourish.

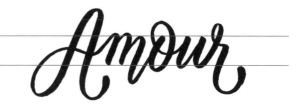

French: Love
Here, the capital *A*, the descender on the lowercase *m*, and the final stroke on the lowercase *r* bounce under the baseline, and the lowercase *o* in the center is opened up and elongated verically.

Letters & Layouts

While it's important to put together the letterforms and create different font styles in the process, the heart of lettering lies in the layout, as you combine words to form a cohesive structure. There are a few key things to remember when it comes to making layouts.

WORD COUNT. A quick tip for beginners: the fewer, the better. Keep in mind that word count helps determine the overall layout of your work and the corresponding font styles that can be used, given how many words your quote has.

GROUPING. Especially when a quote has many words; and it's important to group them together and create a visual hierarchy with corresponding sizes and widths for each word.

ALIGNMENT. Do you want your quote aligned to the left, right, or center? Be sure to allot enough space depending on the alignment you choose.

SPACING. Along with plotting your layout in a structured and organized manner, it's important to allow for white space and enough room for the layout to look cohesive but still be readable.

SPELLING AND GRAMMAR. Always a necessary part of making layouts—double-check your spelling and grammar before beginning your lettering and layouts.

Creating a Layout

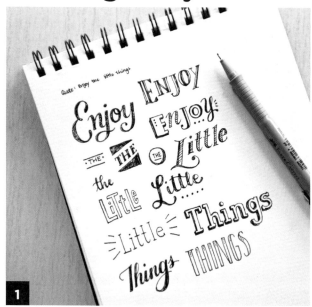

1. COMPILE AND CURATE. From the quote you've selected, create a library of font options in different styles (serif, sans serif, and script). Having this database of font samples can give you a clearer overview in terms of which styles you want to focus on and what font types best suit the words you will letter.

Get creative! Use different font styles and work with the varying structures of words and letters. Choosing and combining font styles are key in coming up with a good layout.

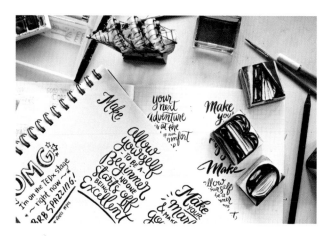

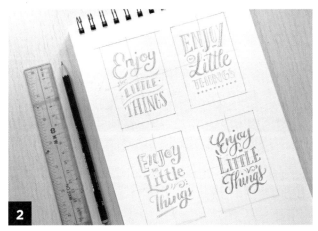

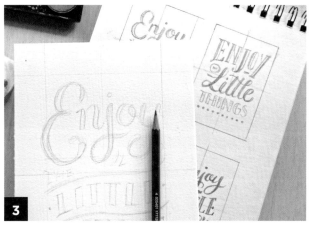

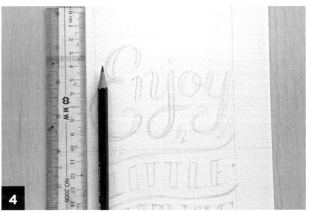

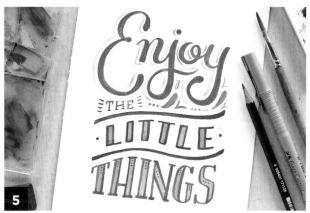

2. COLLECT AND SELECT. Gather a few of your chosen font styles and combine them together in a layout. I like to come up with two to four layouts in thumbnails to experiment and exercise my skills in putting words together. Note that we are still doing the drafts at this point. Keep experimenting and working on your layouts in order to figure out which ones work best for your quote. Also, at this point, think of integrating possible embellishments within the layout.

3. CHOOSE AND COMBINE. Choose one final layout from your thumbnail studies. From there, work on your sample and think of possible color schemes you will use. Make sure to choose at least three to five colors within the same family to ensure that the layout is neat and cohesive.

4. TRANSFER AND PROPORTION. Once your design, color scheme, and layout are finalized, transfer it to your main canvas. Make sure to proportion it properly by creating grid guides so that the work is well balanced. It's recommended that you start your layout in the center, and allow at least 1" (2.5 cm) of white space from all four corners of your paper. This helps create the proper alignment of your work.

5. CREATE AND COLOR. On your final sheet, start filling in your layout with color and add embellishments to your liking. Make sure to keep measurements in check and to maintain cleanliness while working on your piece!

Remember that it takes a lot of practice to make your work look great, but it's always possible if you trust the process and keep working toward improving your illustrations and layouts.

Alternative Letters

Circumflex, Caron & Breve

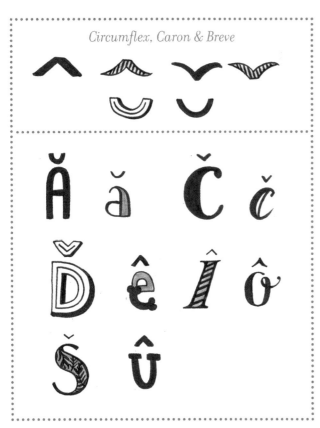

Cedillas, Commas & Ogoneks

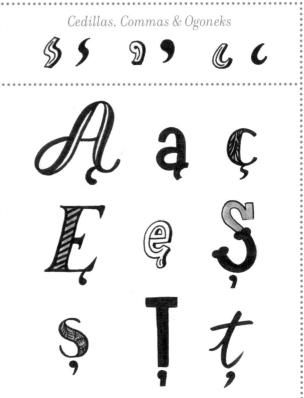

Apostrophes

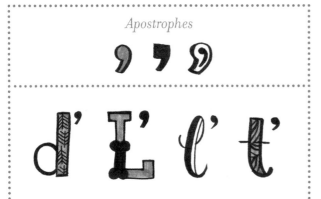

Special Punctuation

Á à Ć

ć É è

ć Ĺ ń ő

Ŕ ś ú

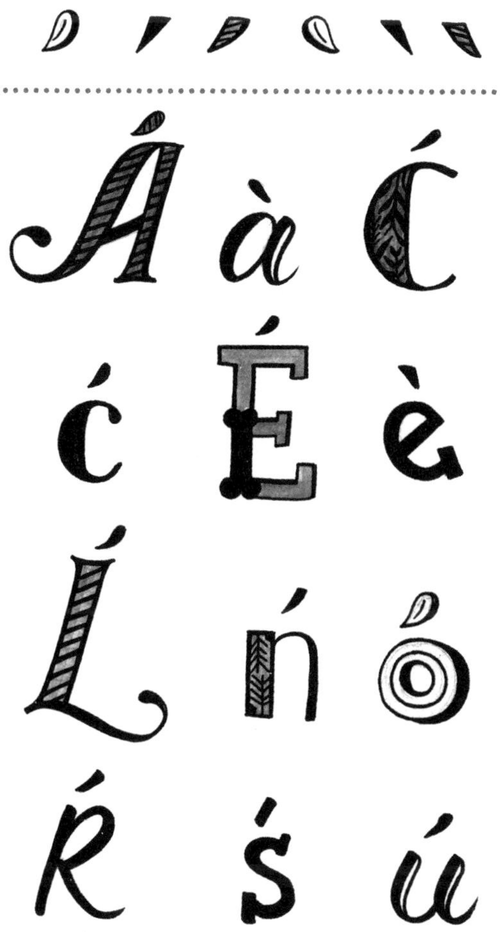

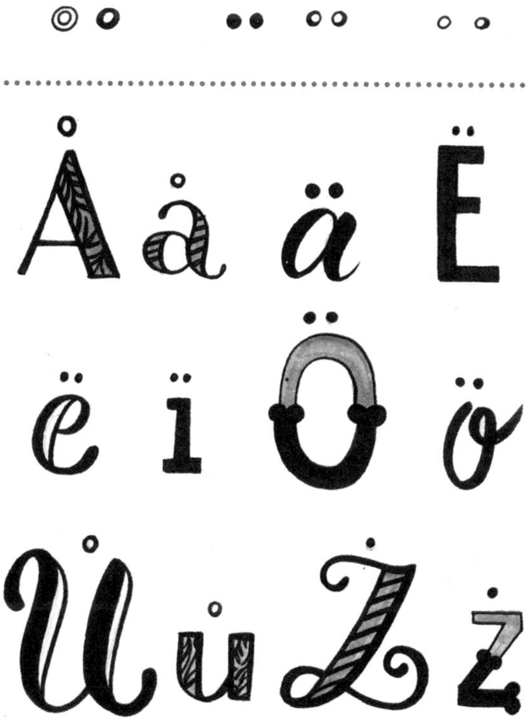

Å å ä Ë

ë ï Ö ö

Ů ü Ž ż

Tilde

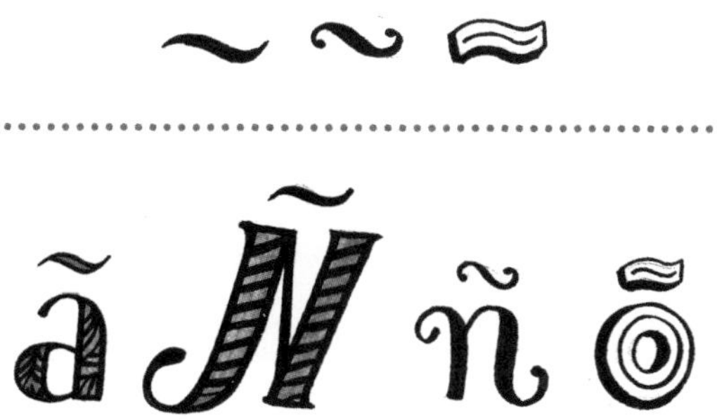

~ ~ ≈

ã Ñ ñ õ

œ Æ æ

ẞ Ŀ Ł

Ø ø

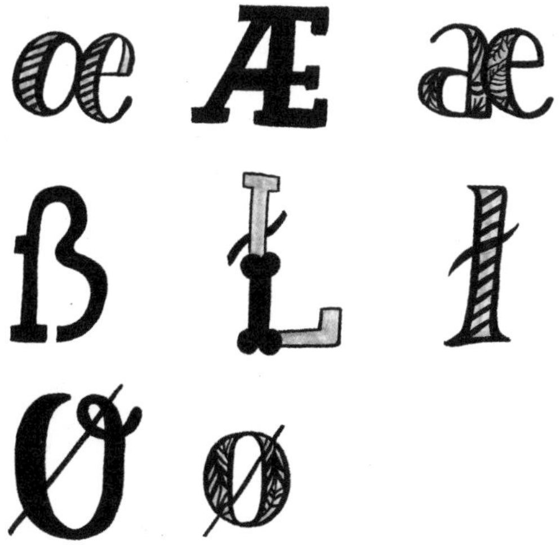

Flourishes & Embellishments

Flourishes add character to your hand-lettering layouts and create a more cohesive look to your design. It's particularly easy to add flourishes to script-style fonts, as they're very fluid and connect well.

You can add flourishes anywhere in your hand-lettering work. Use a flourish to create an extra dimension to a word or quote, as the flourish creates a connective line from the letters to its embellished parts in a layout. Flourishing for modern hand lettering has no definite rules. Keep experimenting with different ways to connect each word and/or letterform and find combinations that work for you.

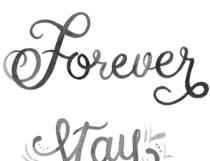

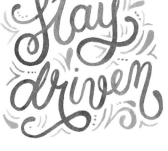

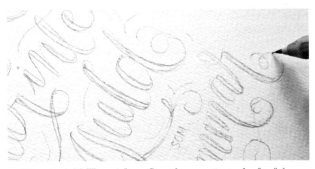

How to Add Flourishes. Start by creating a draft of the quote you will be using. Add bounce, as needed, on a few letters. Find spaces in the layout where flourishes can be added. Experiment with different flourish styles and techniques. Once the layout is seamless, you can start inking it with your brush pen or marker.

Where to Add Flourishes to Words. Anywhere! To the first letter of a word (note the exaggeration of swashes on the *F* in Forever); to a letter in the middle letter of a word, from a hanging tail (on a *g*, *j*, *r*, *s*, *t*, or *y*, for example); or to the last end letter of a word (such as the double loop on the *r* in Forever). For quotes, choose particular letters that can be flourished, and then integrate the flourish with he outside borders for a seamless pattern.

Flowers and Leaves. Here are some samples of flowers and leaves that can be incorporated with letterforms or as additional accents to your layouts. Enhance your lettering work further by incorporating floral borders or wreaths. These create frames and accentuate the lettered phrase.

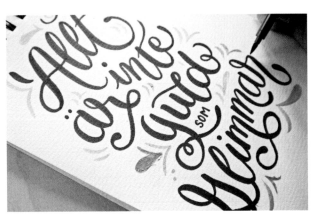

Quote: Allt är inte guld som glimmar.
(German: All that glimmers is not gold.)

Using the Practice Sheets

Regardless of which lettering style you'd like to work on, start by doing the warmup exercises for either the sans serif and serif styles (pages 21 and 23) or the script styles (pages 105 and 107).

On this page and the next, I show two letterforms—one uppercase and one lowercase—from each of the six featured styles. I use them as general examples of how each style is drawn and to point out things to look for or emphasize as you work.

Simple Sans Serif (pages 25–43)

This very simple, basic style is full of creative potential! See page 11 for just a few possible directions. The sky's the limit!

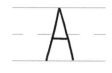 ◀ Work on the main downstrokes before adding the crossbars.

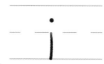 ◀ For this style, stick with simple, straightforward strokes to warm up.

Embellished Sans Serif (pages 45–63)

The letterforms in this loose, casual style are worked directly with a brush marker, then embellished with a fineliner.

 ◀ Start with a thick downstroke, then use thinner upstrokes to create curved forms.

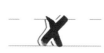 ◀ Note how the thick and thin variations create a distinction between the two strokes.

Simple Serif (pages 65–83)

This style can be drawn directly with a marker or outlined in pencil and then filled in with colors and/or patterns.

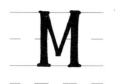 ◀ The main downstrokes are thicker; stems and crossbars are thinner.

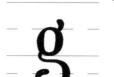 ◀ Be sure to add brackets or ball terminals to the ends of the strokes.

Swash Serif (pages 85–103)

These letterforms start with a penciled outline that can then be embellished with various color, designs, or illustrations.

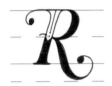 ◀ The exaggerated swashes end with a ball terminal.

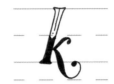 ◀ Note that many of the swashes extend well below the baseline.

Simple Script (pages 109–127)

This easy, direct style can be worked precisely (as shown in the practice sheets) or "bounce" slightly to exceed top and bottom guidelines (as in the exemplar on page 109).

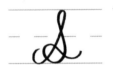 ◀ This letter S follows the traditional script style; feel free to change it up with a modern S.

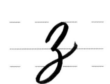 ◀ Some lowercase letters, such as m, n, o, y, and z, are scaled-down version of their uppercase counterparts.

Simple Script (pages 109–127)

This whimsical style adds curves and curls to a basic script. See also pages 163 and 165 for more flourishes.

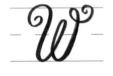 ◀ Notice the loop between the two Us in W—this gives the letterform a more rounded and distinct look.

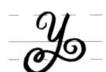 ◀ To create a double loop, start with your downstroke, then complete it by adding another circular stroke inside it.

SANS SERIF/SERIF WARMUPS

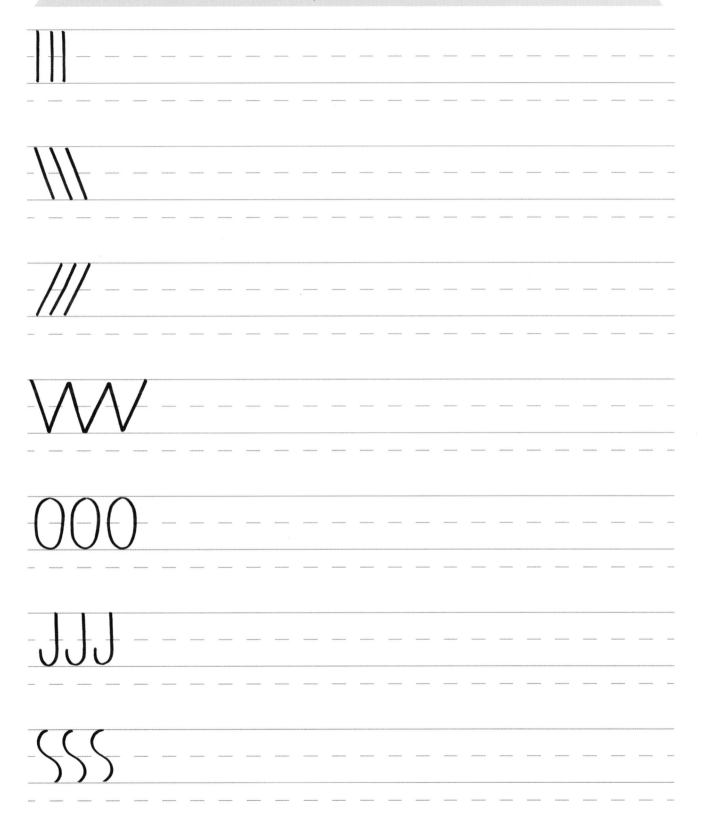

Place tracing paper over sheet or remove and photocopy

III

III

III

WW

OOO

JJJ

SSS

Place tracing paper over sheet or remove and photocopy

Aa Bb Cc Dd Ee

Ff Gg Hh Ii Jj

Kk Ll Mm Nn Oo

Pp Qq Rr Ss

Tt Uu Vv Ww

Xx Yy Zz !?&

1234567890

Place tracing paper over sheet or remove and photocopy

a

b

c

d

e

f

g

Place tracing paper over sheet or remove and photocopy

h

i

j

k

l

m

n

Place tracing paper over sheet or remove and photocopy

o

p

q

r

s

t

u

Place tracing paper over sheet or remove and photocopy

V

W

X

y

z

A

B

Place tracing paper over sheet or remove and photocopy

C

D

E

F

G

H

I

Place tracing paper over sheet or remove and photocopy

J

K

L

M

N

O

P

Place tracing paper over sheet or remove and photocopy

Q

R

S

T

U

V

W

Place tracing paper over sheet or remove and photocopy

X

Y

Z

1

2

3

4

Place tracing paper over sheet or remove and photocopy

5

6

7

8

9

0

1   ?   &

Place tracing paper over sheet or remove and photocopy

Aa Bb Cc Dd

Ee Ff Gg Hh Ii

Jj Kk Ll Mm Nn

Oo Pp Qq Rr Ss

Tt Uu Vv Ww

Xx Yy Zz ! & ?

0 1 2 3 4 5 6 7 8 9

Place tracing paper over sheet or remove and photocopy

a

b

c

d

e

f

g

Place tracing paper over sheet or remove and photocopy

h

i

j

k

l

m

n

Place tracing paper over sheet or remove and photocopy

o

p

q

r

s

t

u

Place tracing paper over sheet or remove and photocopy

v

w

x

y

z

A

B

Place tracing paper over sheet or remove and photocopy

C

D

E

F

G

H

I

Place tracing paper over sheet or remove and photocopy

J

K

L

M

N

O

P

Place tracing paper over sheet or remove and photocopy

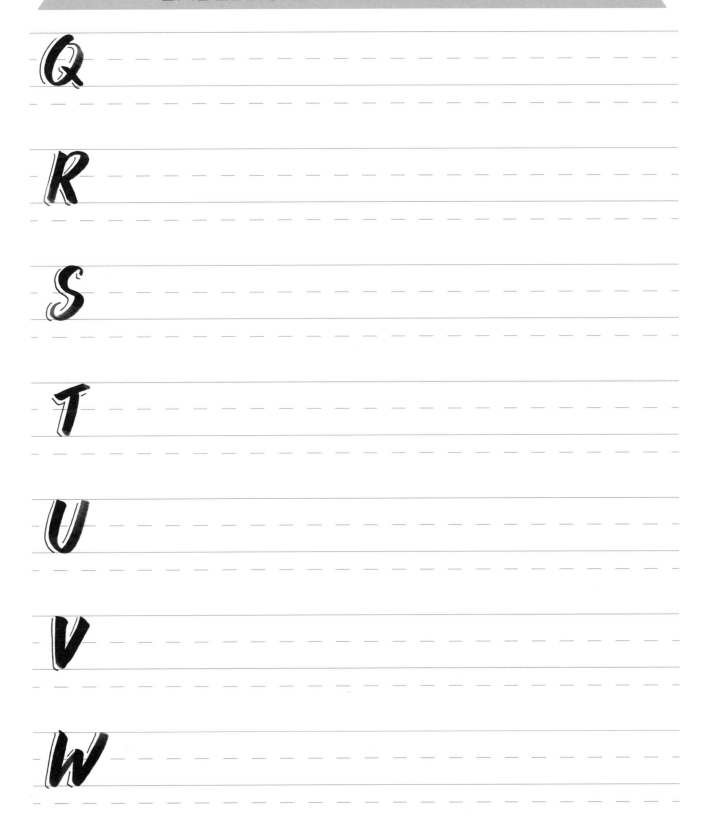

Place tracing paper over sheet or remove and photocopy

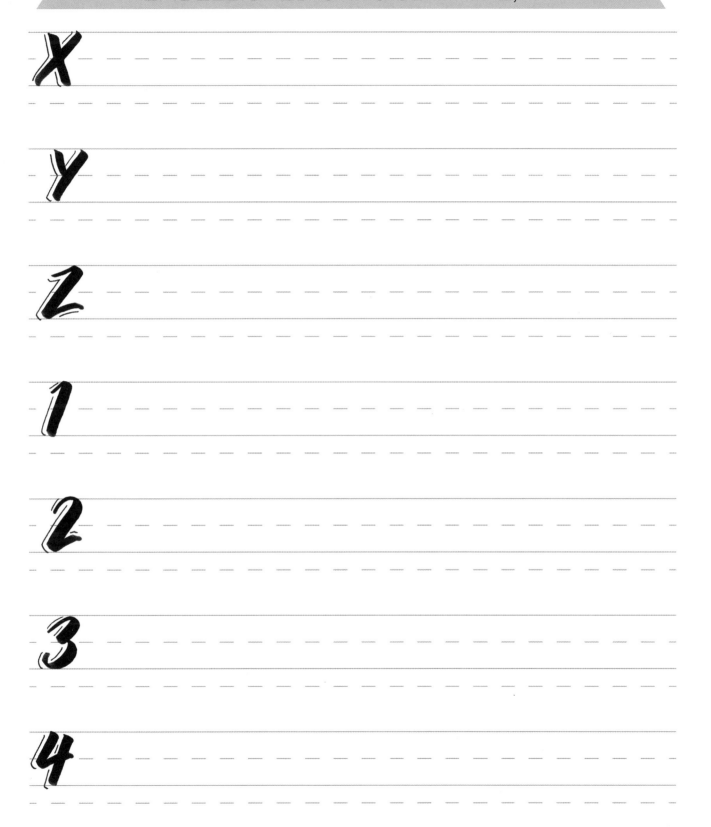

Place tracing paper over sheet or remove and photocopy

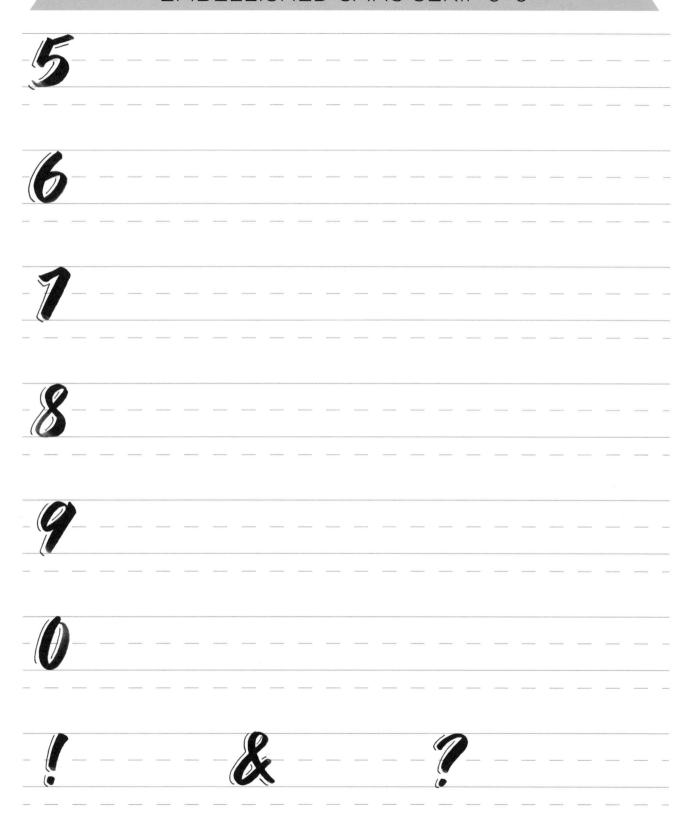

Place tracing paper over sheet or remove and photocopy

Aa Bb Cc Dd Ee Ff

Gg Hh Ii Jj Kk Ll

Mm Nn Oo Pp Qq

Rr Ss Tt Uu Vv

Ww Xx Yy Zz

1234567

890!?&

Place tracing paper over sheet or remove and photocopy

a

b

c

d

e

f

g

Place tracing paper over sheet or remove and photocopy

h

i

j

k

l

m

n

Place tracing paper over sheet or remove and photocopy

o

p

q

r

s

t

u

Place tracing paper over sheet or remove and photocopy

V

W

X

Y

Z

A

B

Place tracing paper over sheet or remove and photocopy

C

D

E

F

G

H

I

Place tracing paper over sheet or remove and photocopy

J

K

L

M

N

O

P

Place tracing paper over sheet or remove and photocopy

Q

R

S

T

U

V

W

Place tracing paper over sheet or remove and photocopy

X

Y

Z

1

2

3

4

Place tracing paper over sheet or remove and photocopy

5

6

7

8

9

0

!   ?   &

Place tracing paper over sheet or remove and photocopy

Aa Bb Cc Dd Ee

Ff Gg Hh Ii Jj

Kk Ll Mm

Nn Oo Pp Qq Rr

Ss Tt Uu Vv

Ww Xx Yy Zz

1 2 3 4 5 6 7 8 9 0 ! ? &

Place tracing paper over sheet or remove and photocopy

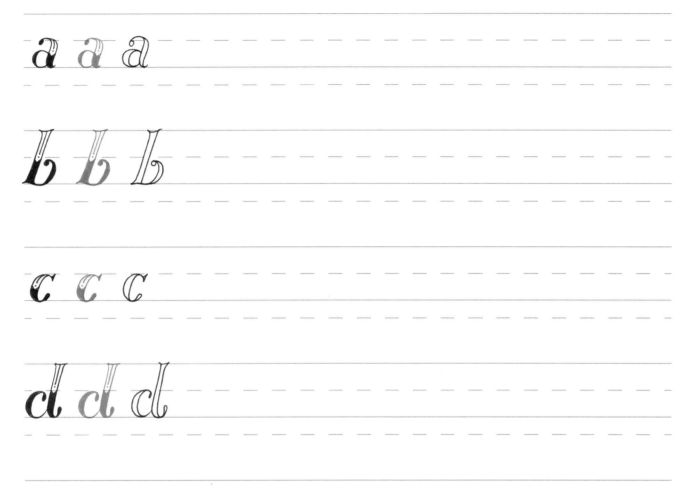

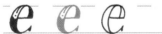

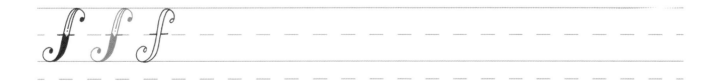

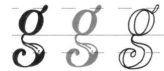

Place tracing paper over sheet or remove and photocopy

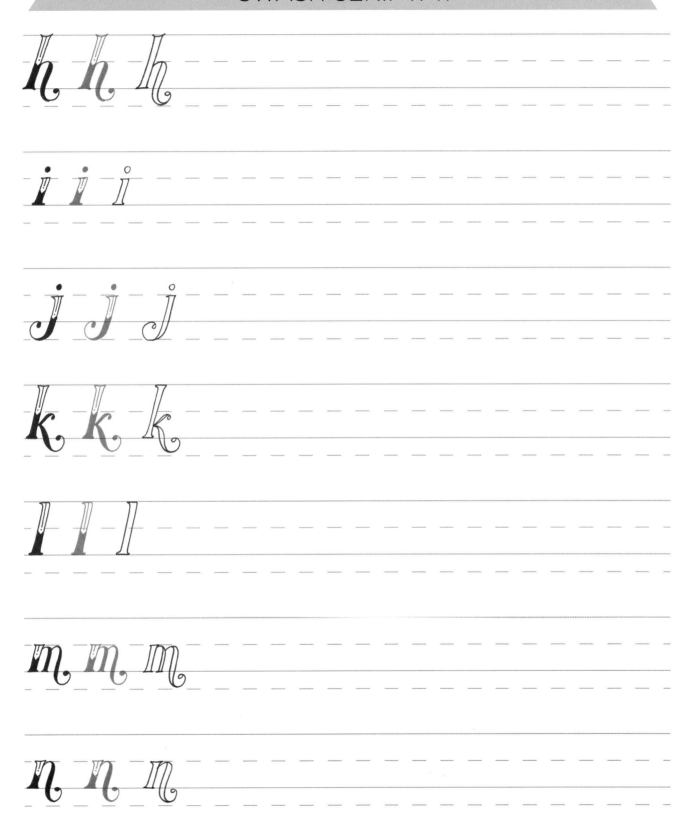

Place tracing paper over sheet or remove and photocopy

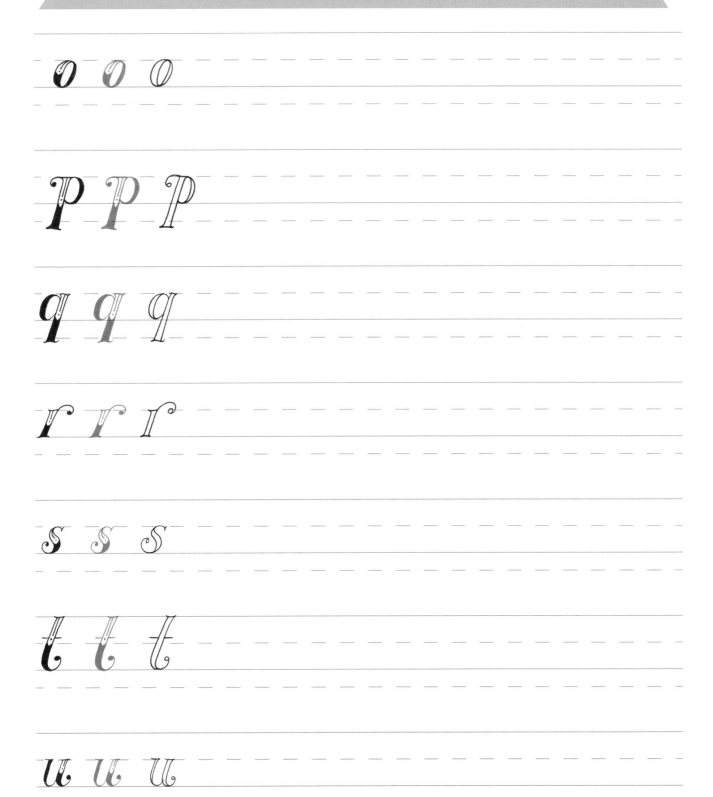

Place tracing paper over sheet or remove and photocopy

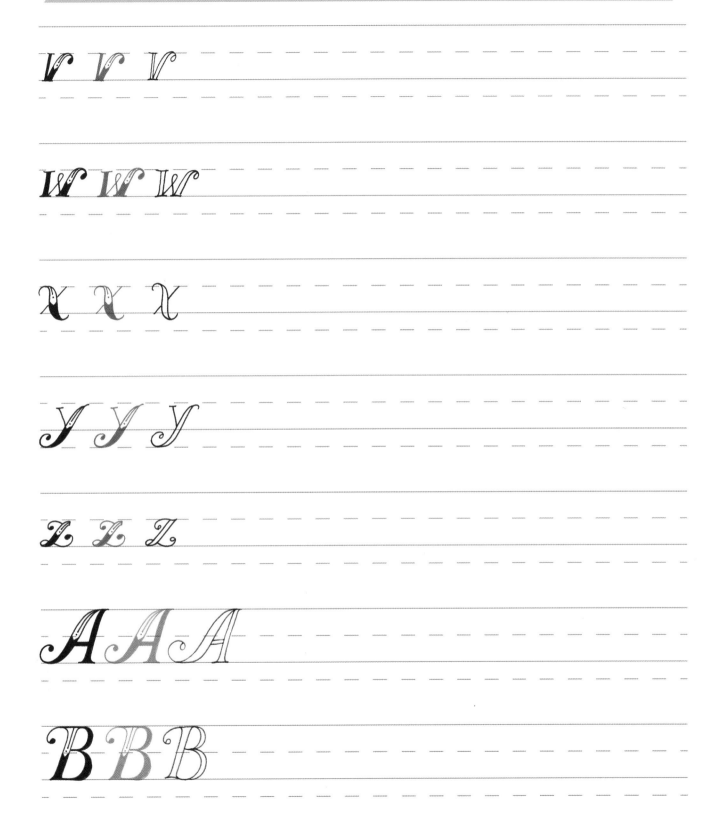

Place tracing paper over sheet or remove and photocopy

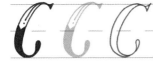

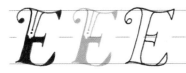

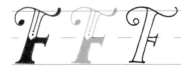

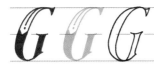

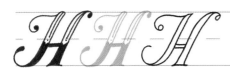

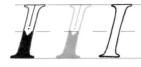

Place tracing paper over sheet or remove and photocopy

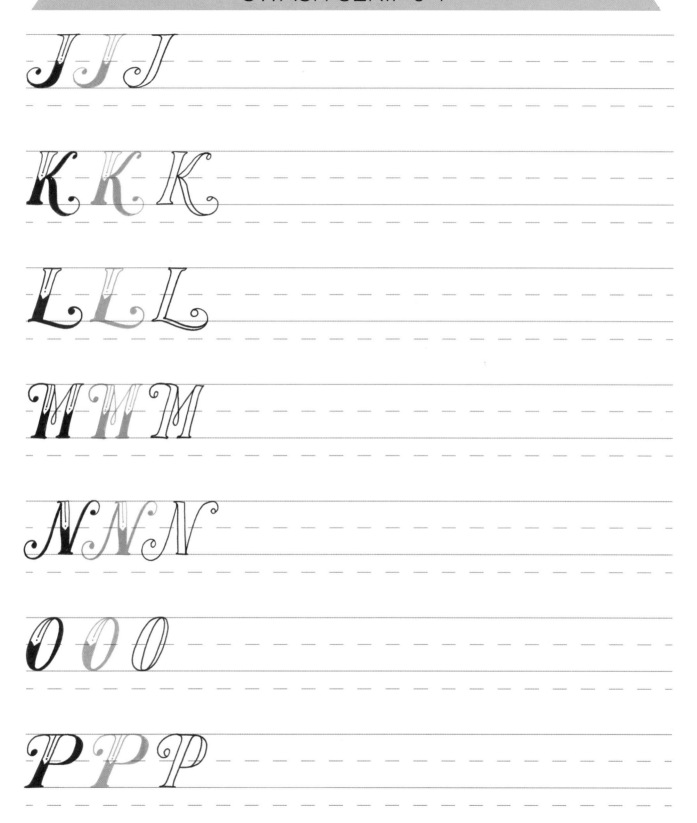

Place tracing paper over sheet or remove and photocopy

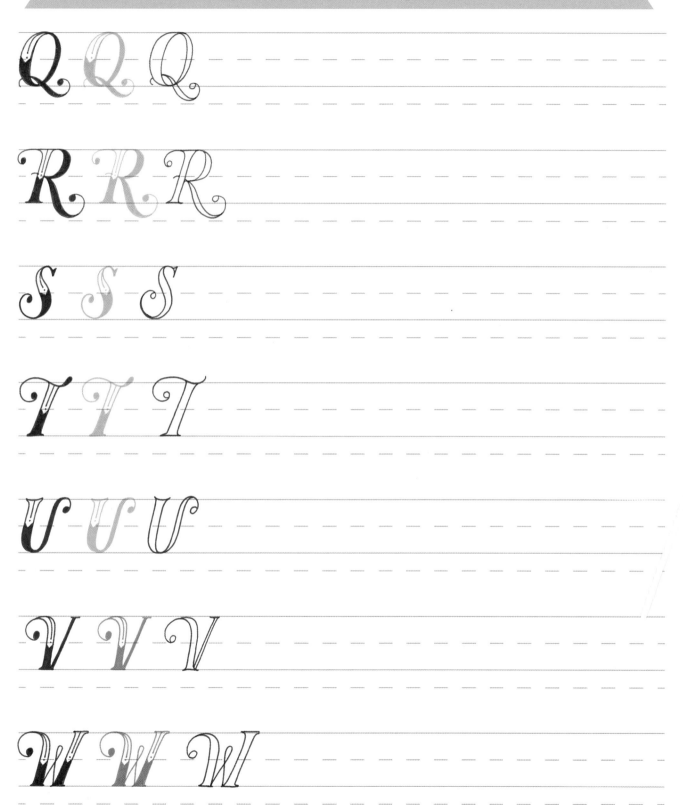

Place tracing paper over sheet or remove and photocopy

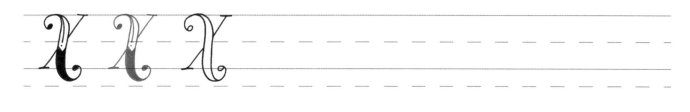

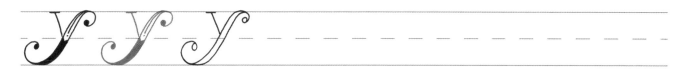

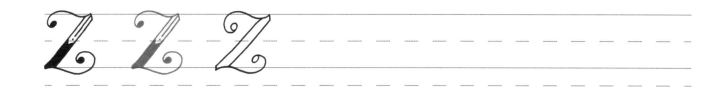

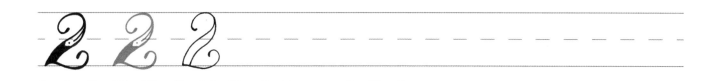

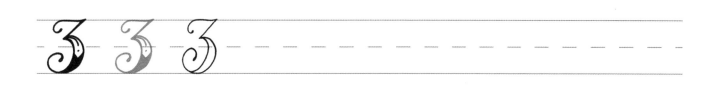

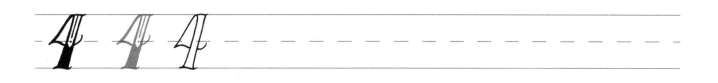

Place tracing paper over sheet or remove and photocopy

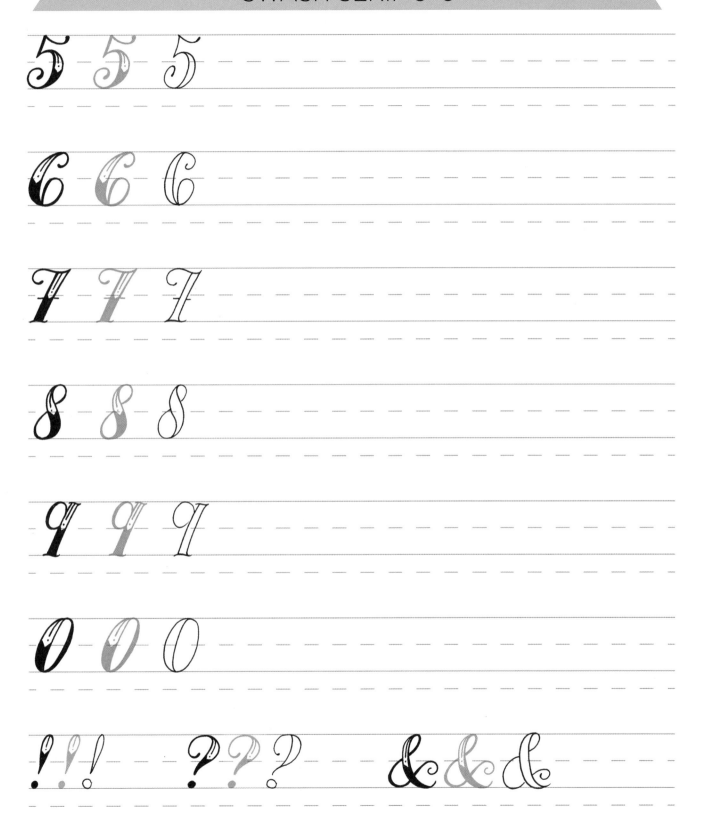

Place tracing paper over sheet or remove and photocopy

SCRIPT WARMUPS

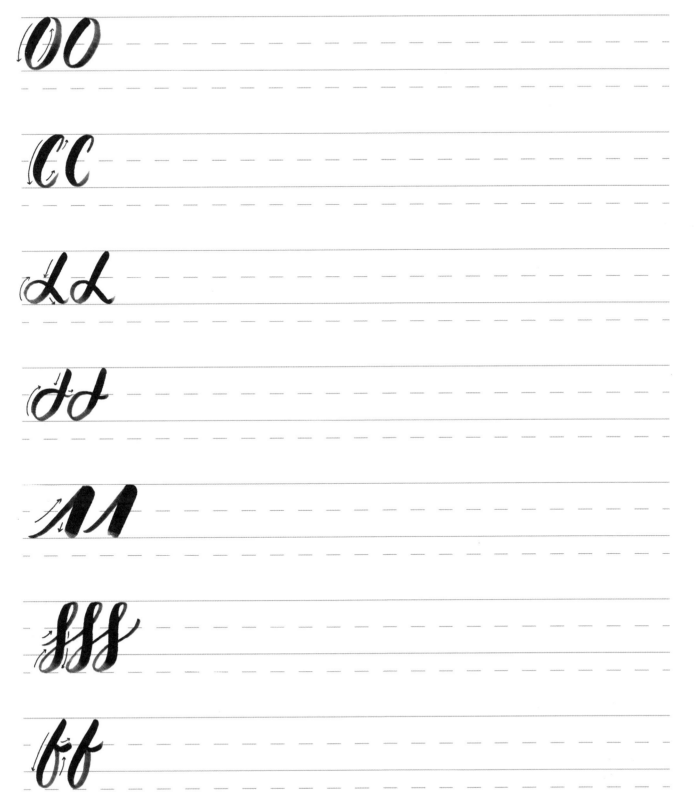

Place tracing paper over sheet or remove and photocopy

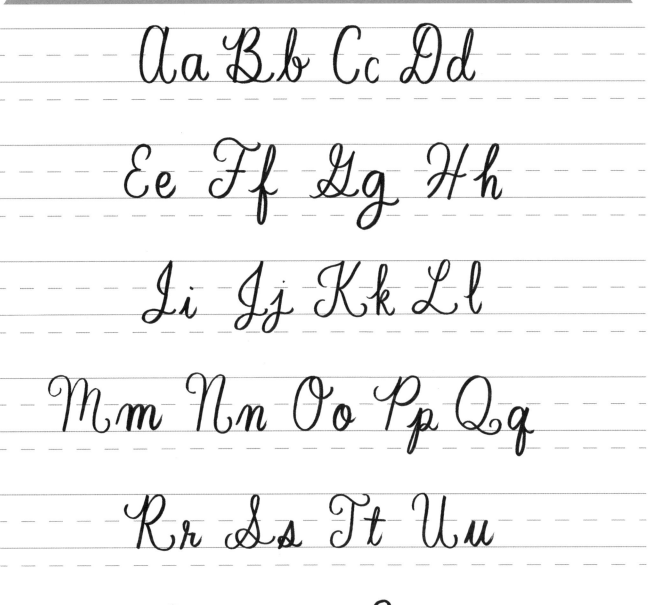

Place tracing paper over sheet or remove and photocopy

a

b

c

d

e

f

g

Place tracing paper over sheet or remove and photocopy

h

i

j

k

l

m

n

Place tracing paper over sheet or remove and photocopy

o

p

q

r

s

t

u

Place tracing paper over sheet or remove and photocopy

v

w

x

y

z

a

B

Place tracing paper over sheet or remove and photocopy

C

D

E

F

G

H

I

Place tracing paper over sheet or remove and photocopy

J

K

L

M

N

O

P

Place tracing paper over sheet or remove and photocopy

Q

R

S

T

U

V

W

Place tracing paper over sheet or remove and photocopy

X

y

3

1

2

3

4

Place tracing paper over sheet or remove and photocopy

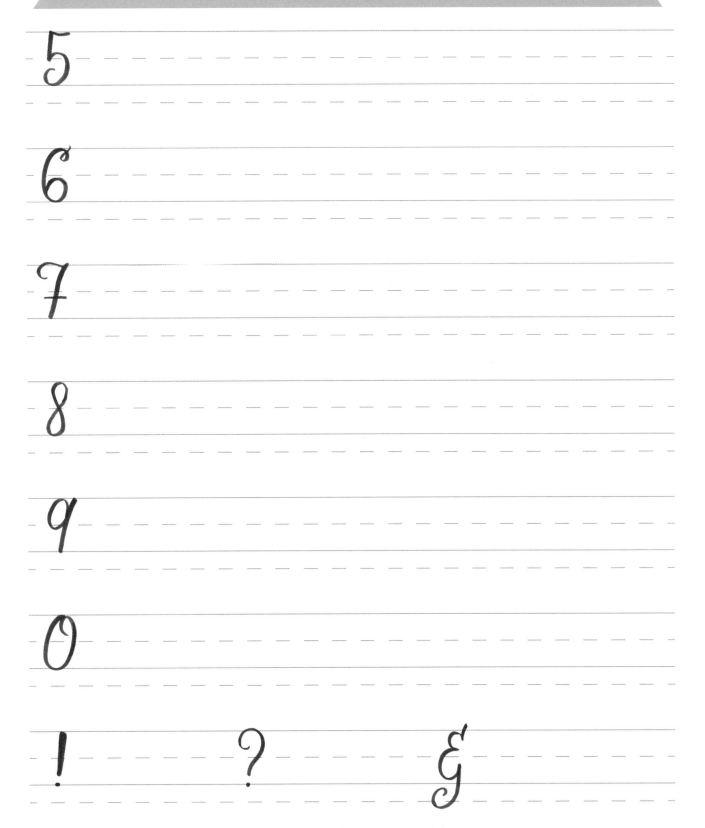

Place tracing paper over sheet or remove and photocopy

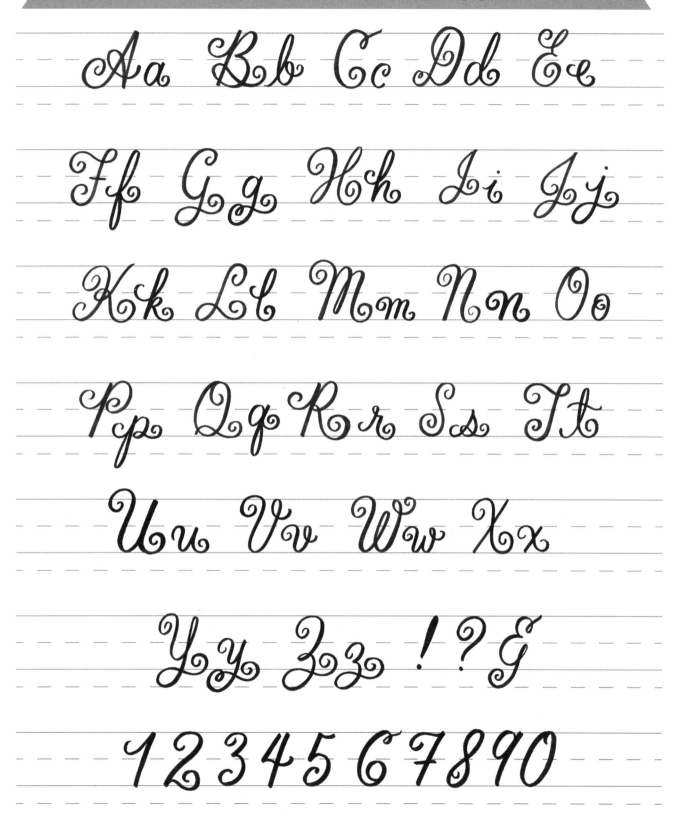

Place tracing paper over sheet or remove and photocopy

a

b

c

d

e

f

g

Place tracing paper over sheet or remove and photocopy

h

i

j

k

l

m

n

Place tracing paper over sheet or remove and photocopy

o

p

q

r

s

t

u

Place tracing paper over sheet or remove and photocopy

v

w

x

y

z

A

B

Place tracing paper over sheet or remove and photocopy

C

D

E

F

G

H

I

Place tracing paper over sheet or remove and photocopy

J

K

L

M

N

O

P

Place tracing paper over sheet or remove and photocopy

Q

R

S

T

U

V

W

Place tracing paper over sheet or remove and photocopy

X

Y

Z

1

2

3

4

Place tracing paper over sheet or remove and photocopy

5

6

7

8

9

0

!   ?   G

Place tracing paper over sheet or remove and photocopy

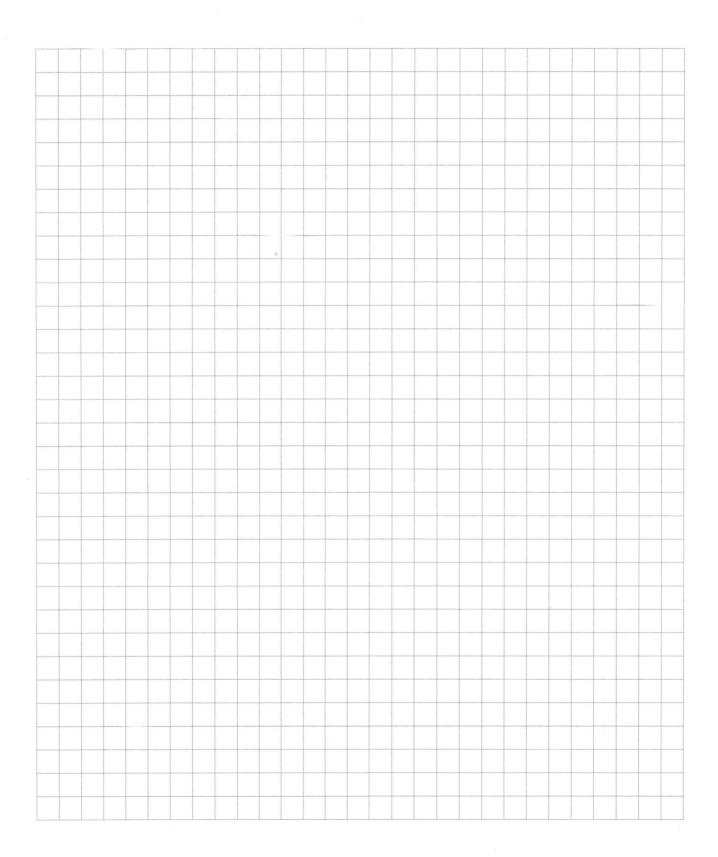

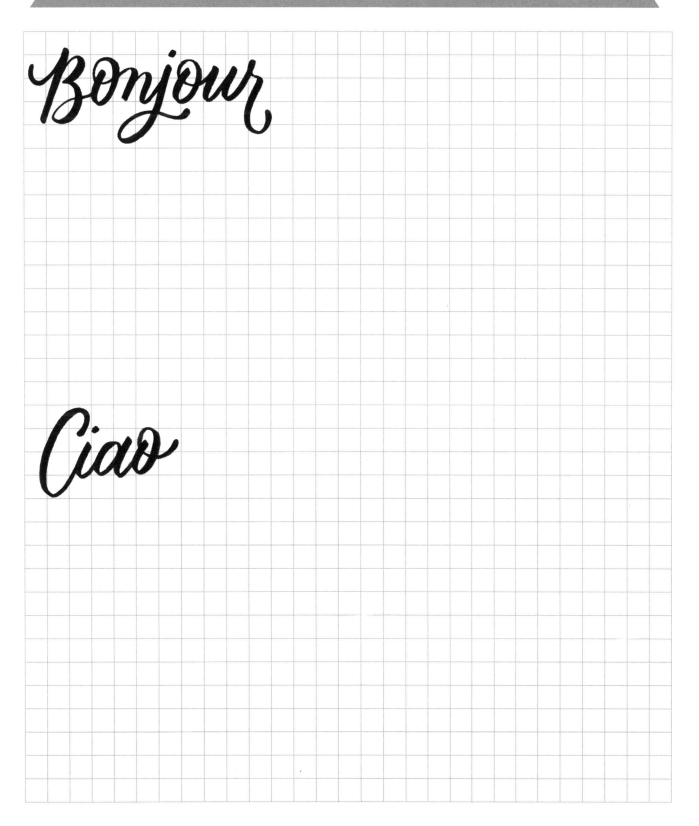

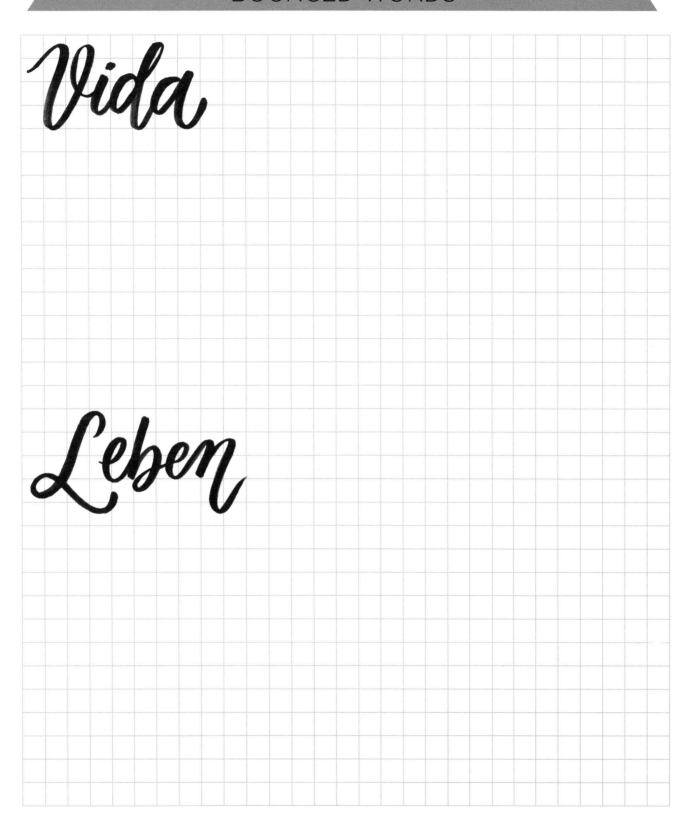

Vida

Leben

Place tracing paper over sheet or remove and photocopy

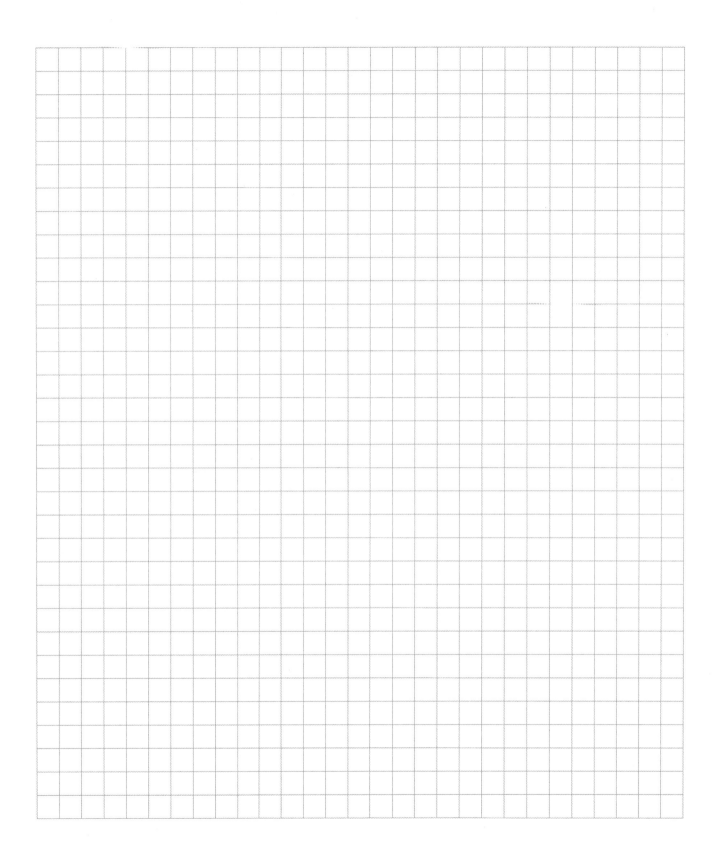

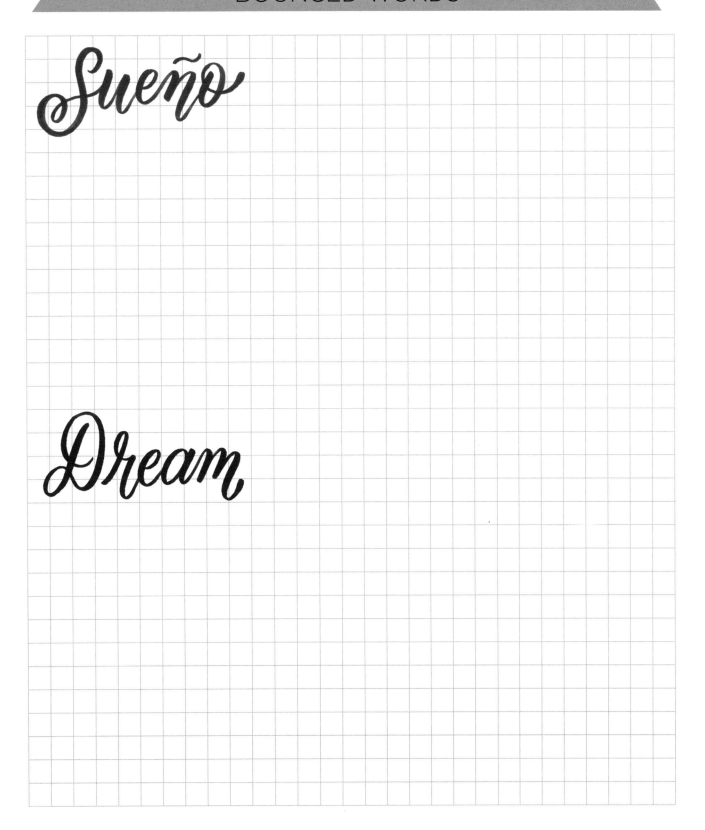

Sueño

Dream

Place tracing paper over sheet or remove and photocopy

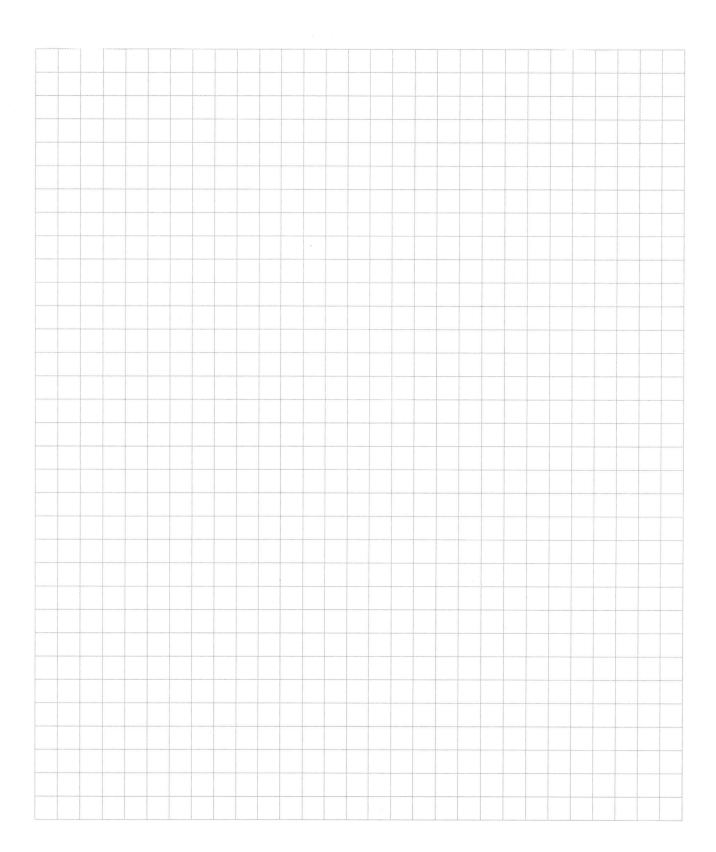

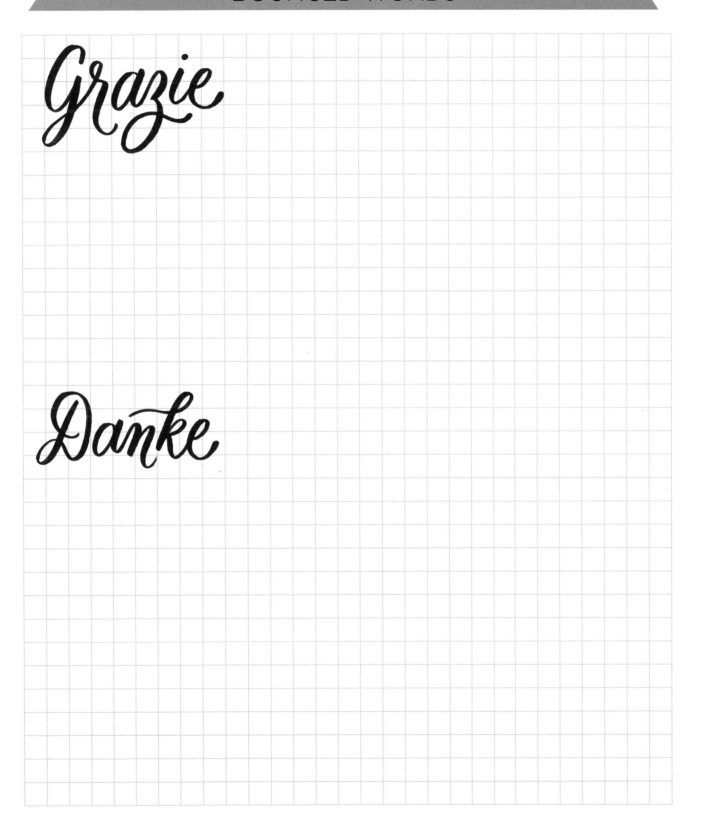

Grazie

Danke

Place tracing paper over sheet or remove and photocopy

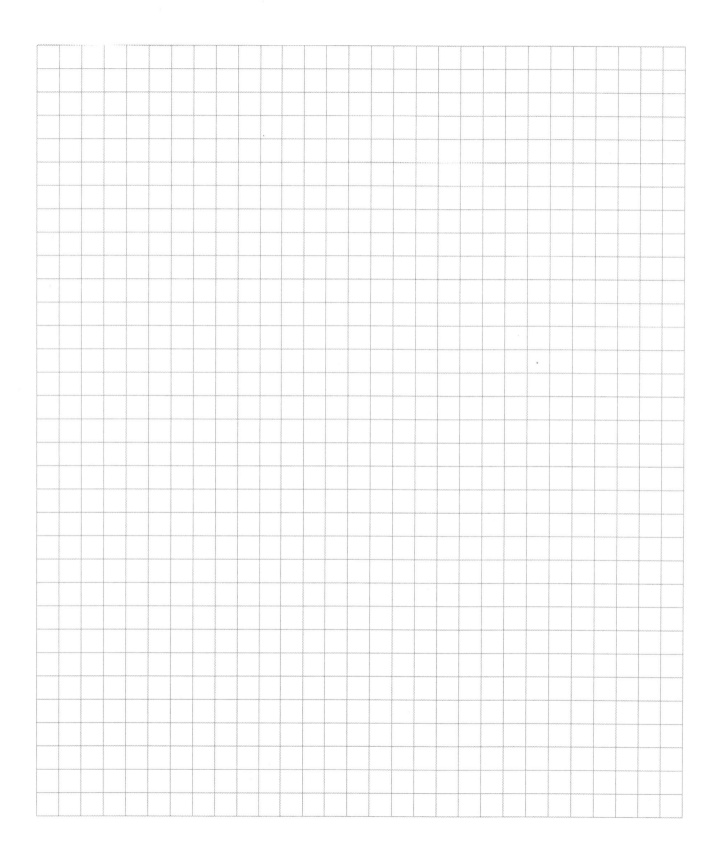

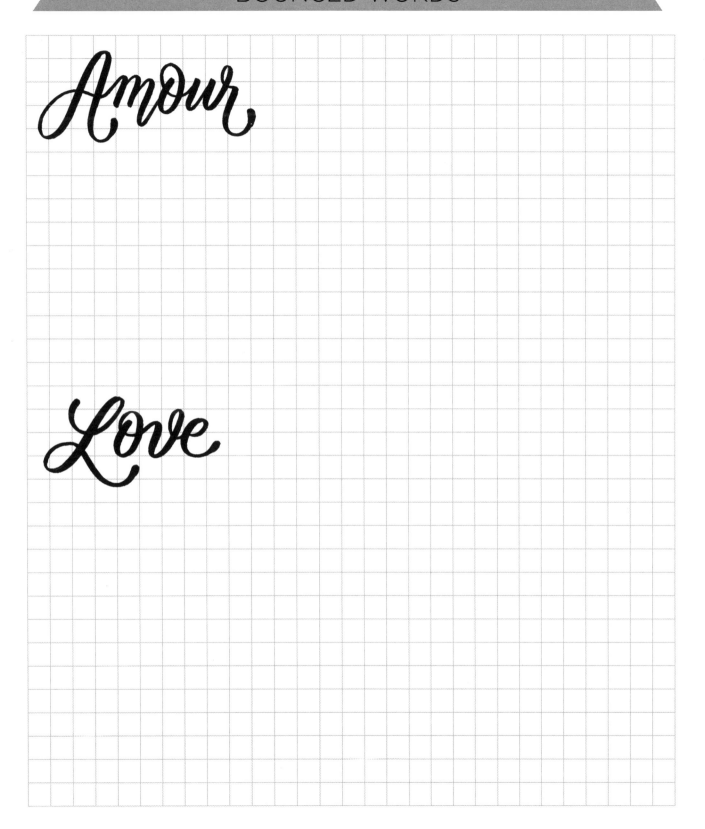

Place tracing paper over sheet or remove and photocopy

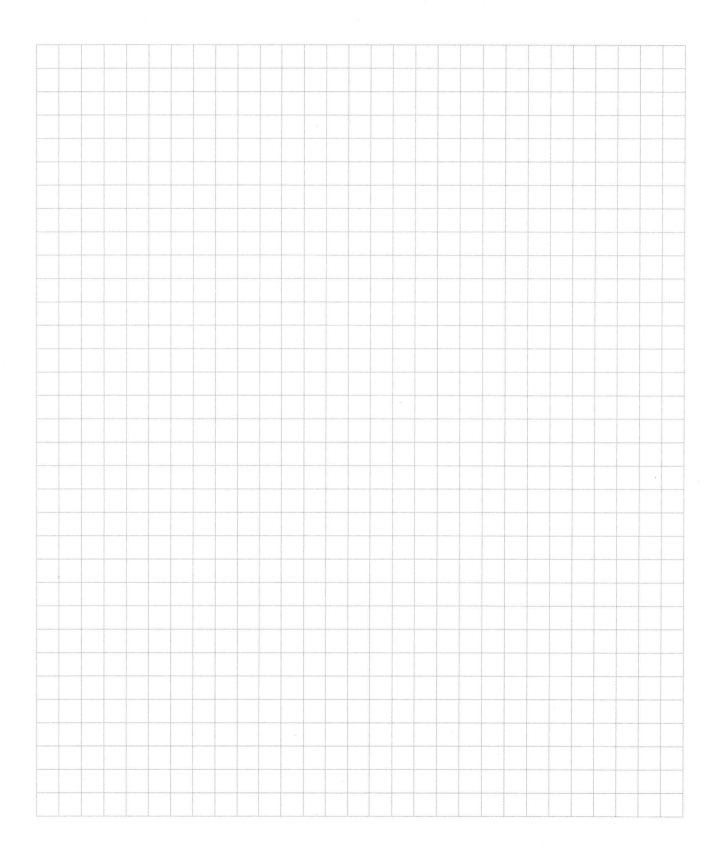

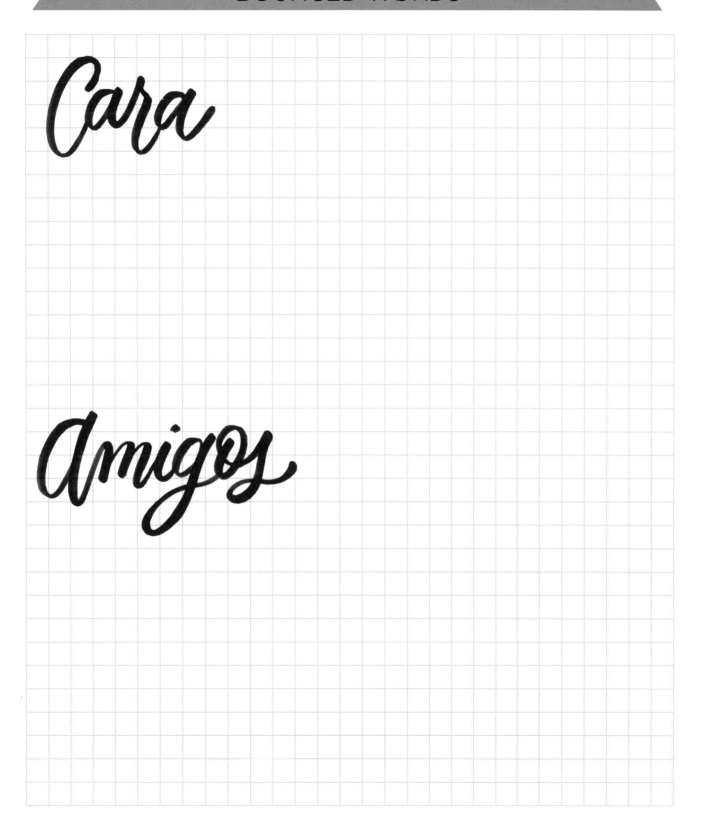

Place tracing paper over sheet or remove and photocopy

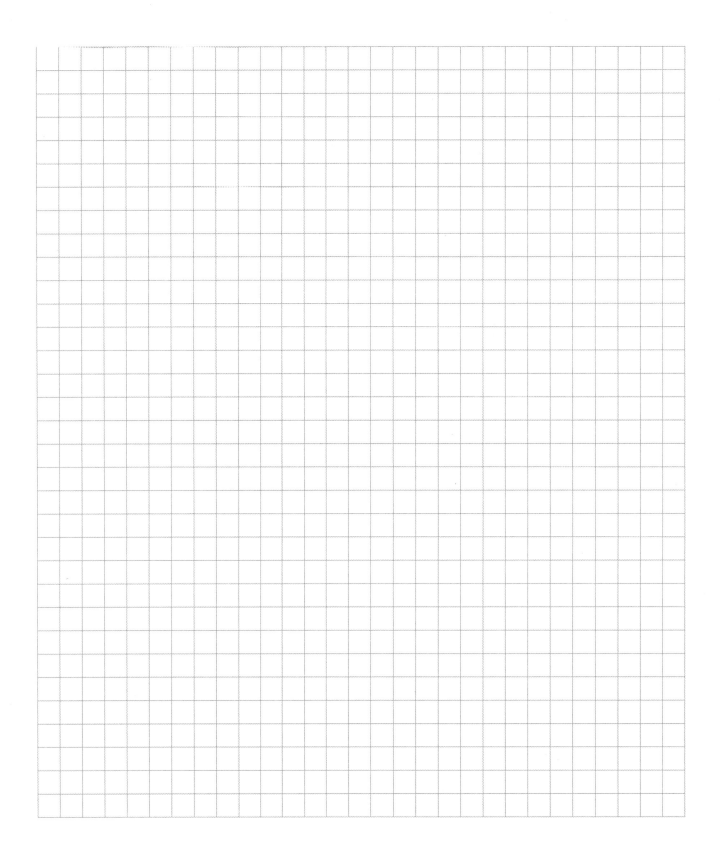

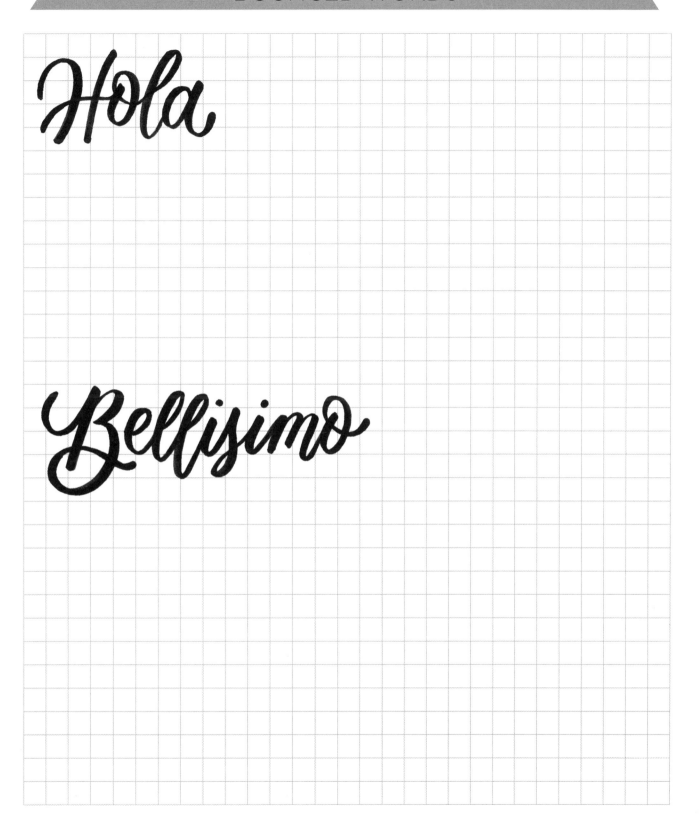

Hola

Bellisimo

Place tracing paper over sheet or remove and photocopy

Place tracing paper over sheet or remove and photocopy

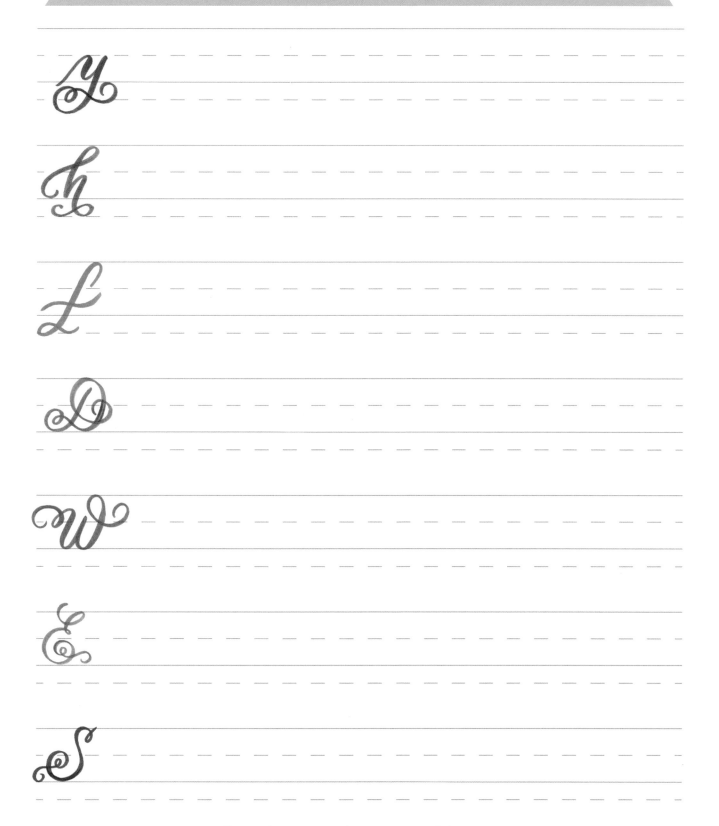

Place tracing paper over sheet or remove and photocopy

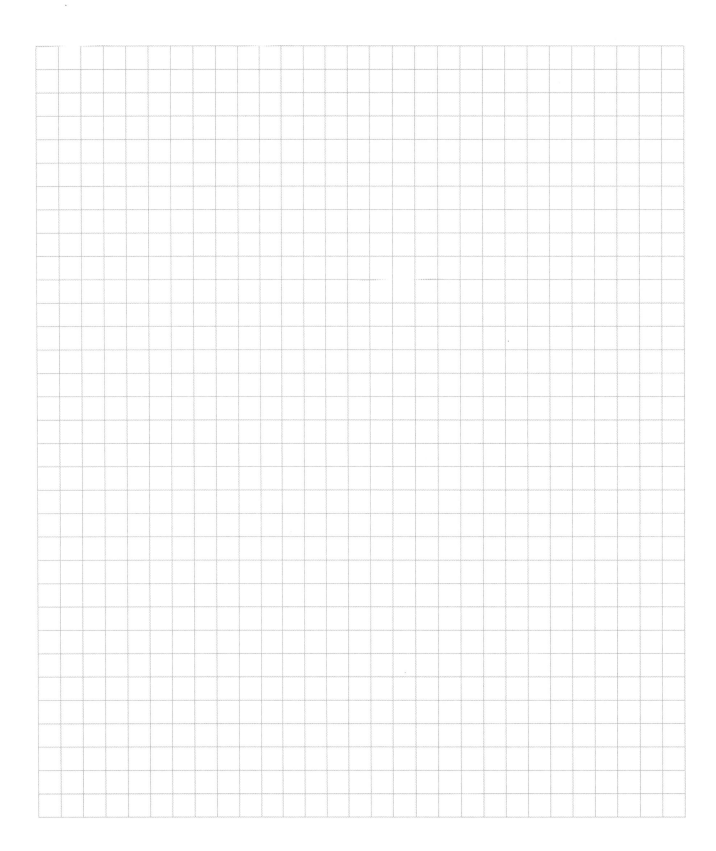

Place tracing paper over sheet or remove and photocopy

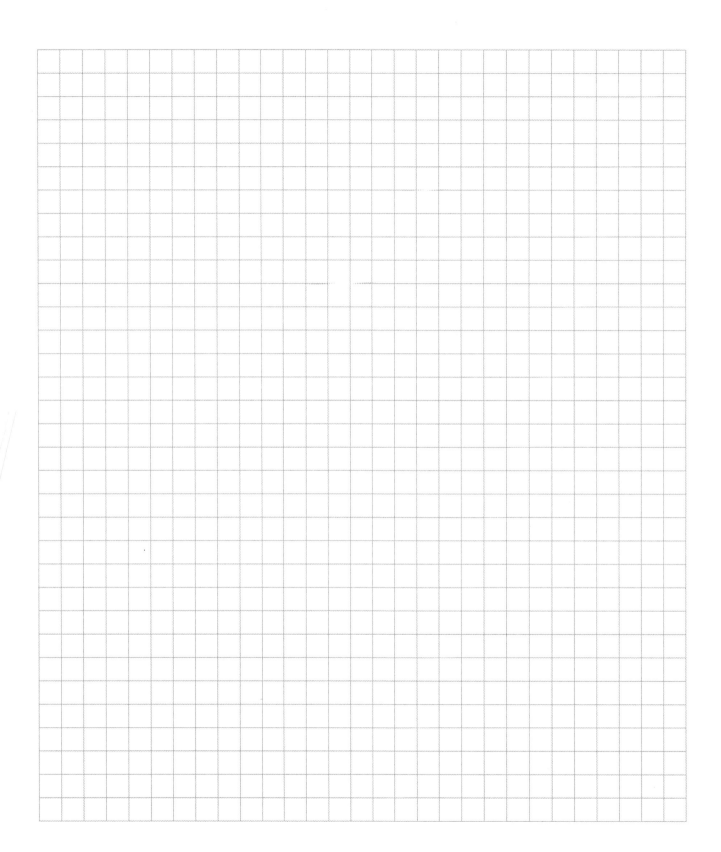

Place tracing paper over sheet or remove and photocopy

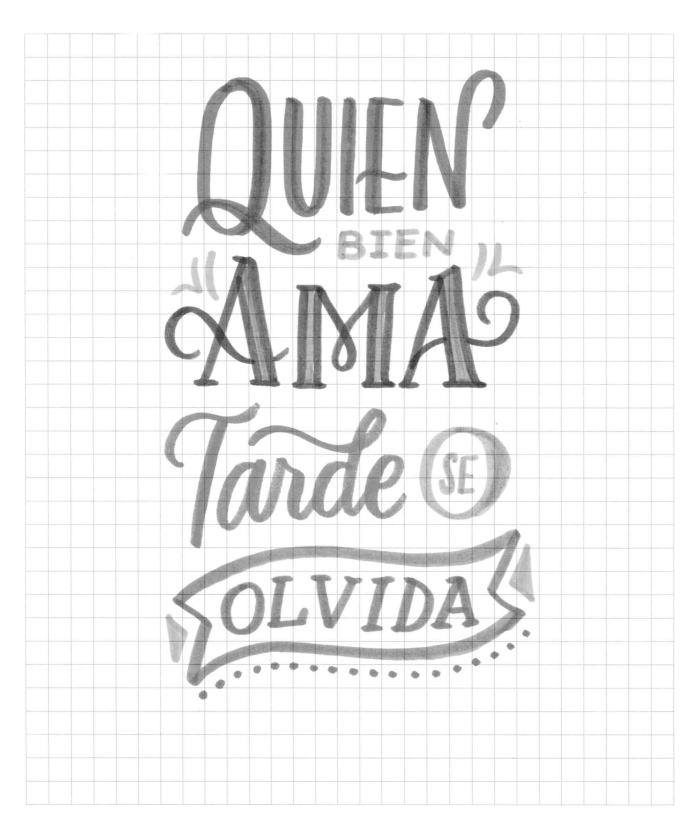

Spanish: True love never grows old

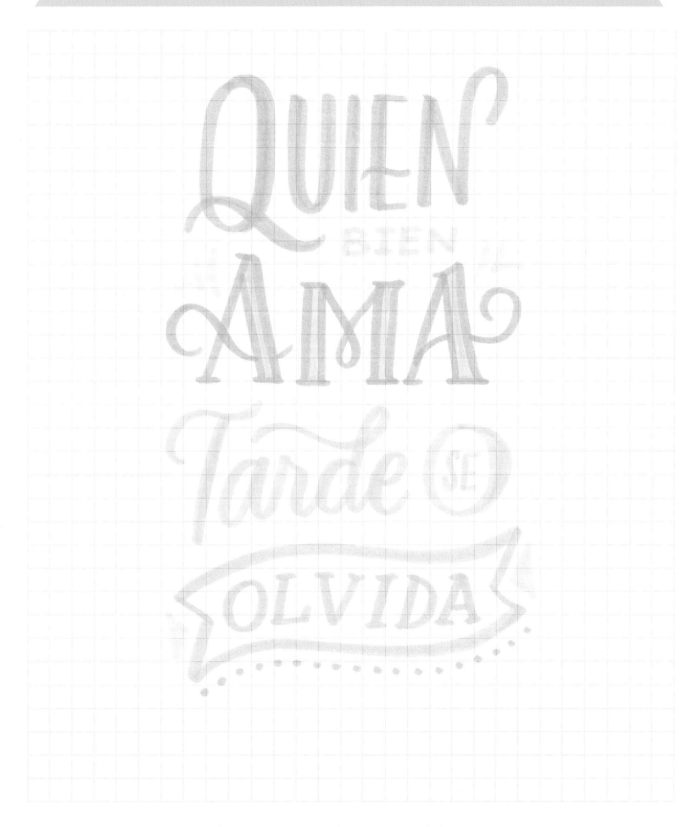

Place tracing paper over sheet or remove and photocopy

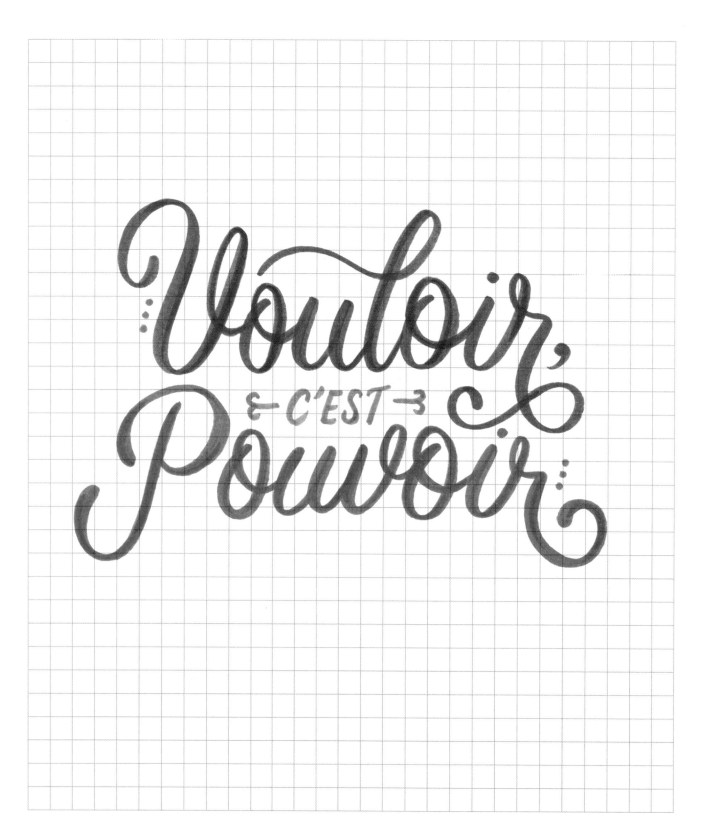

French: Where there's a will, there's a way

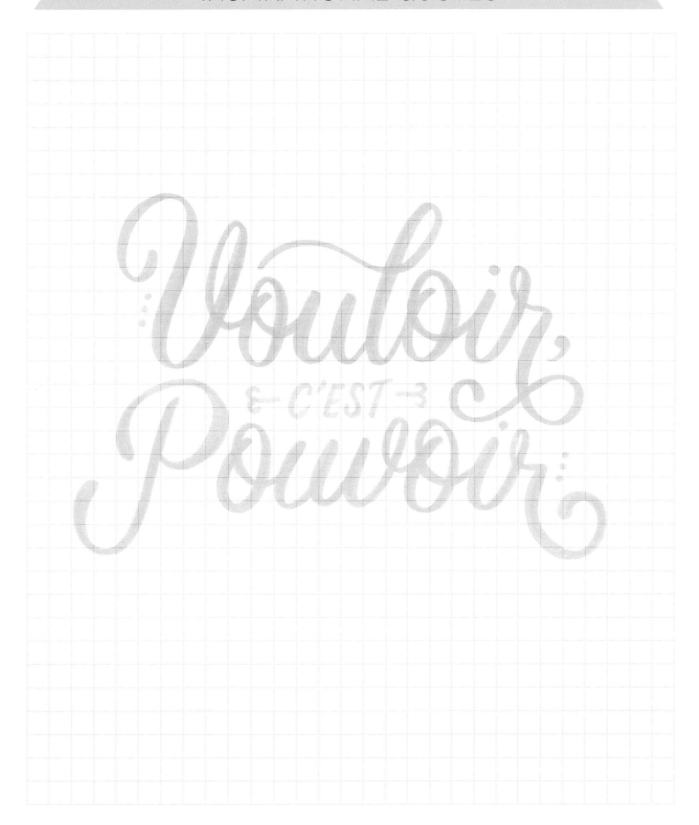

Place tracing paper over sheet or remove and photocopy

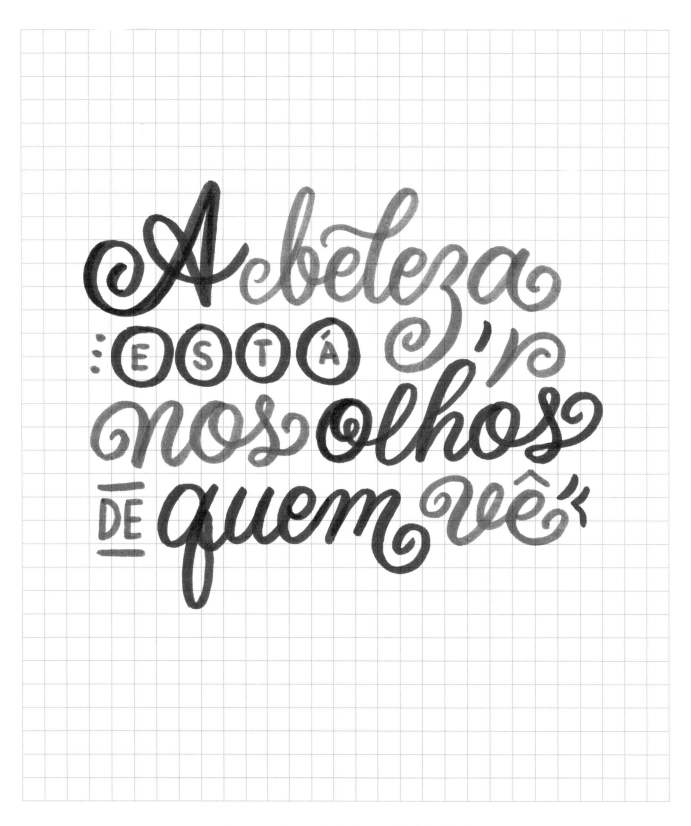

Portuguese: Beauty lies in the eye of the beholder

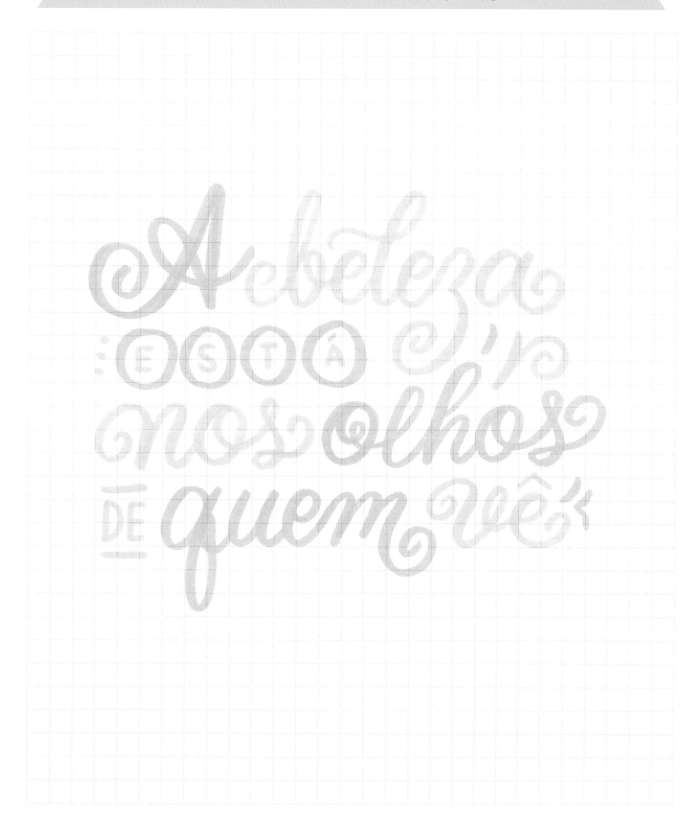

Place tracing paper over sheet or remove and photocopy

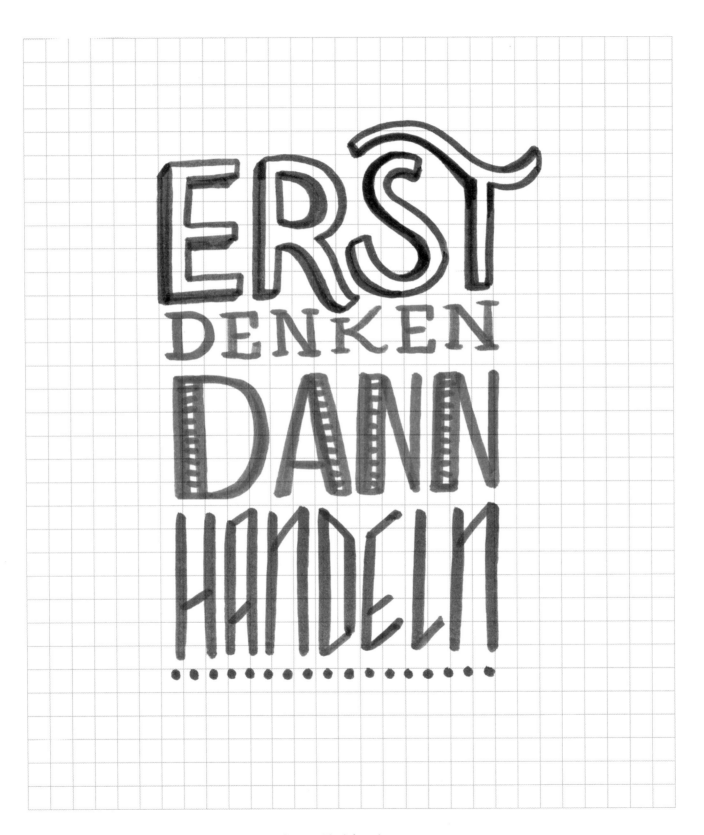

German: Think first, then act

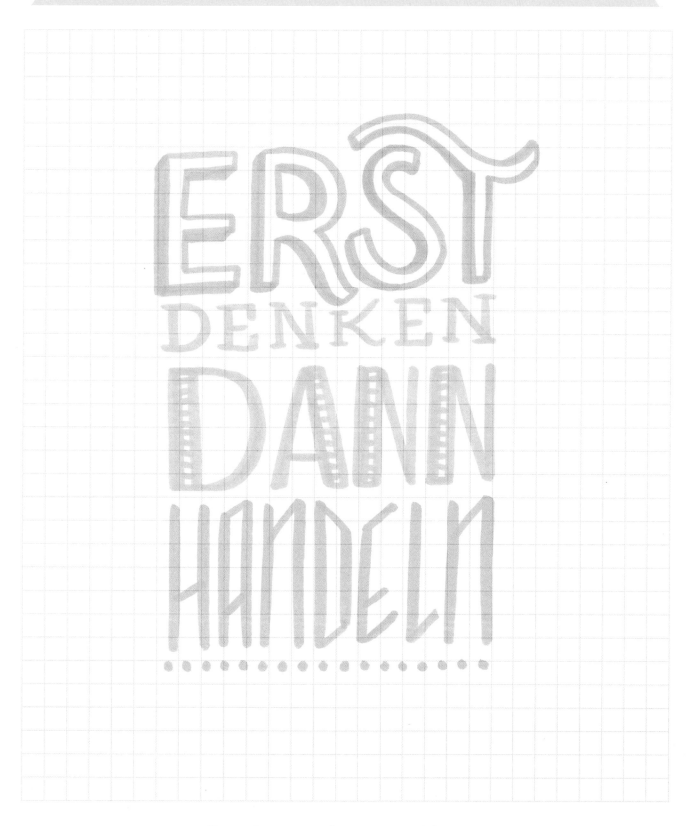

Place tracing paper over sheet or remove and photocopy

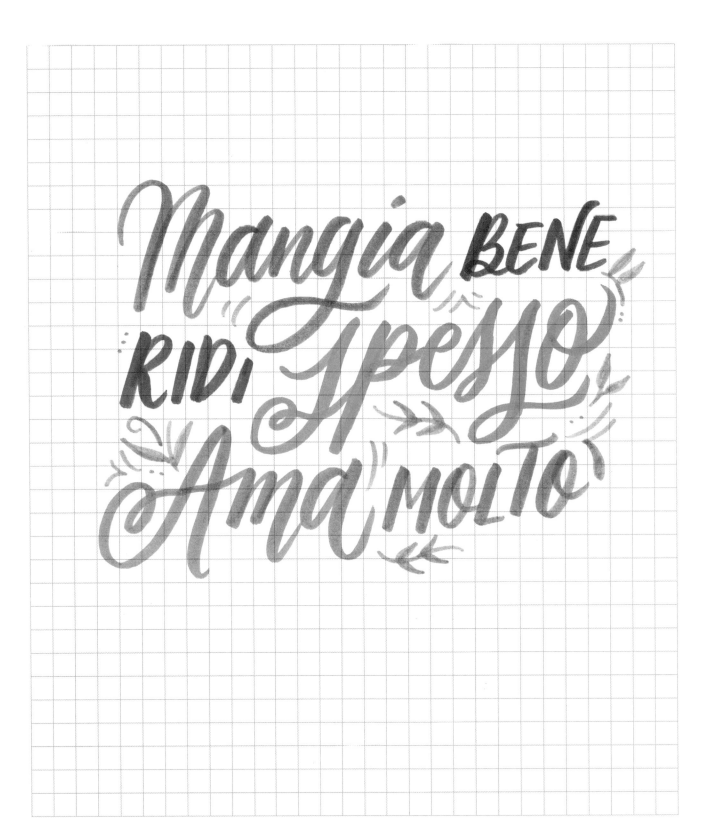

Italian: Eat well, laugh often, love much

Place tracing paper over sheet or remove and photocopy

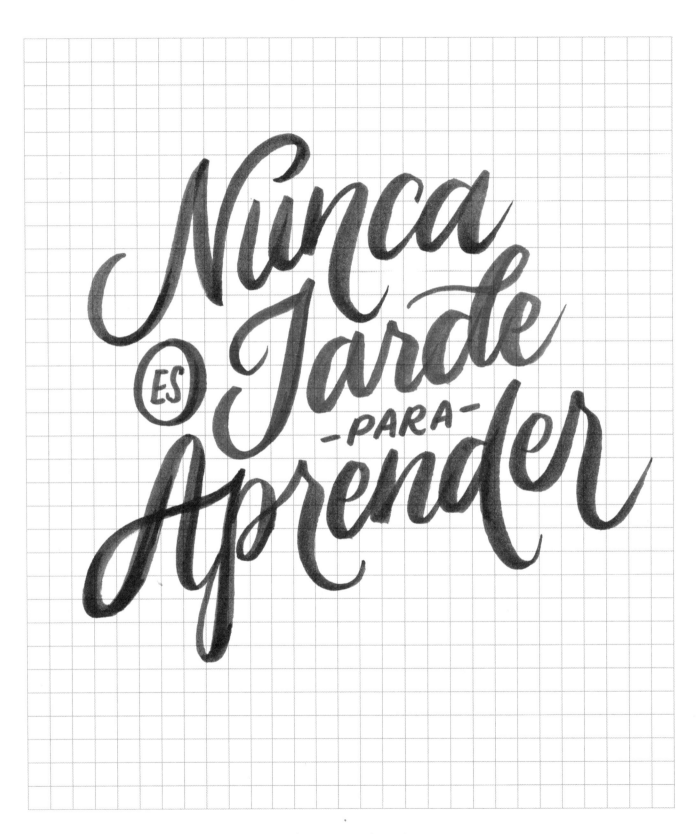

Spanish: It's never too late to learn

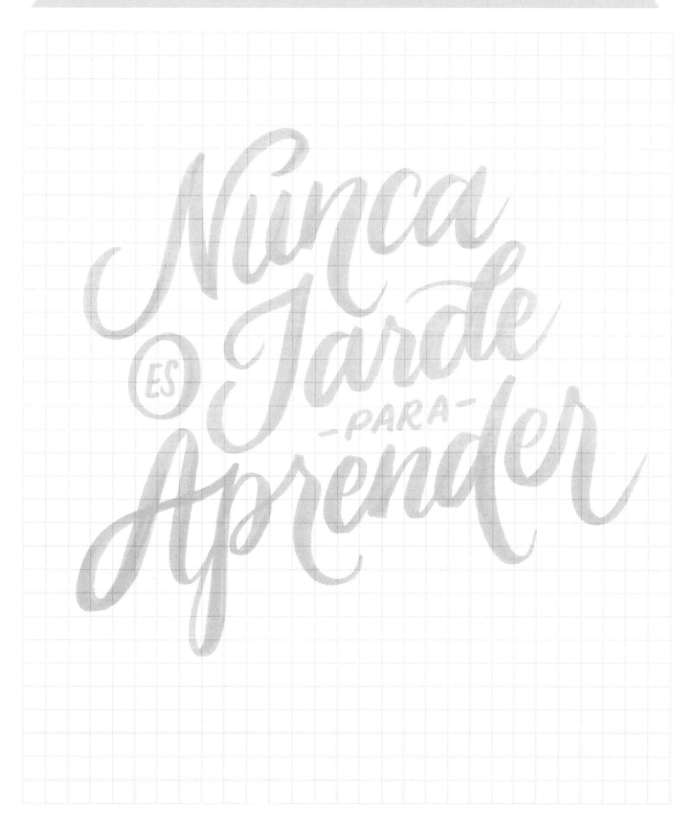

Place tracing paper over sheet or remove and photocopy

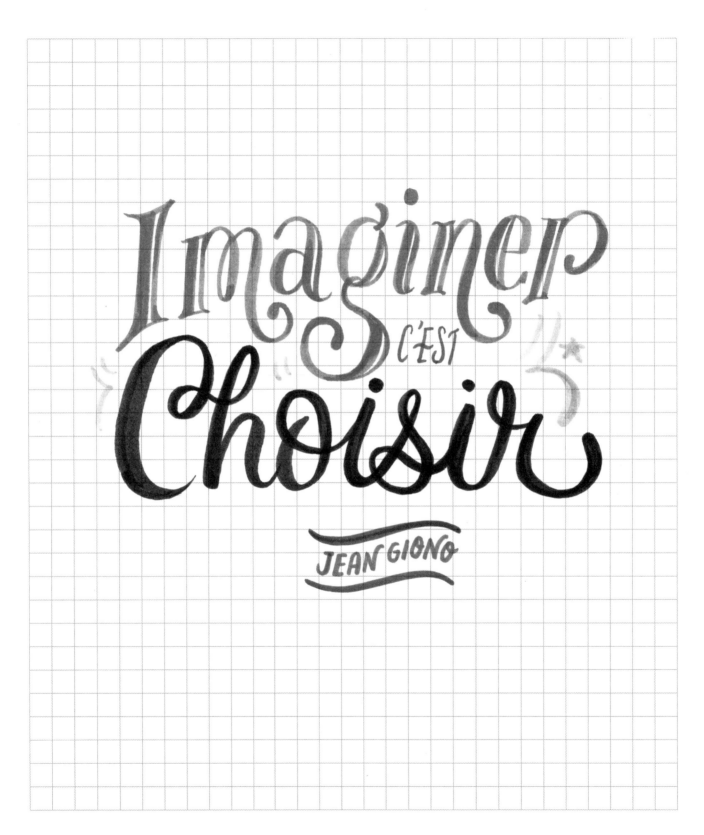

French: To imagine is to choose. —Jean Giono

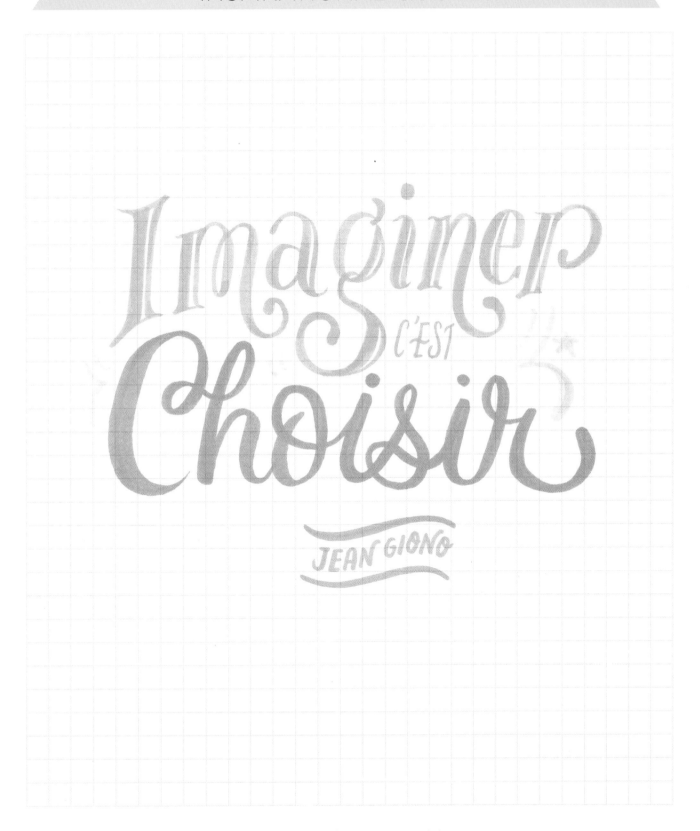

Place tracing paper over sheet or remove and photocopy

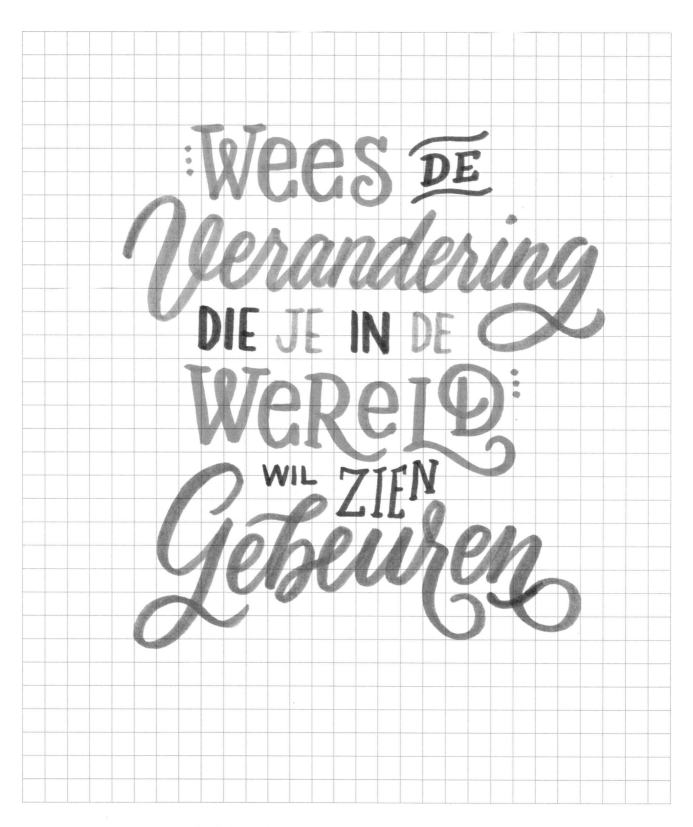

Dutch: Be the change you want to see happening in the world.

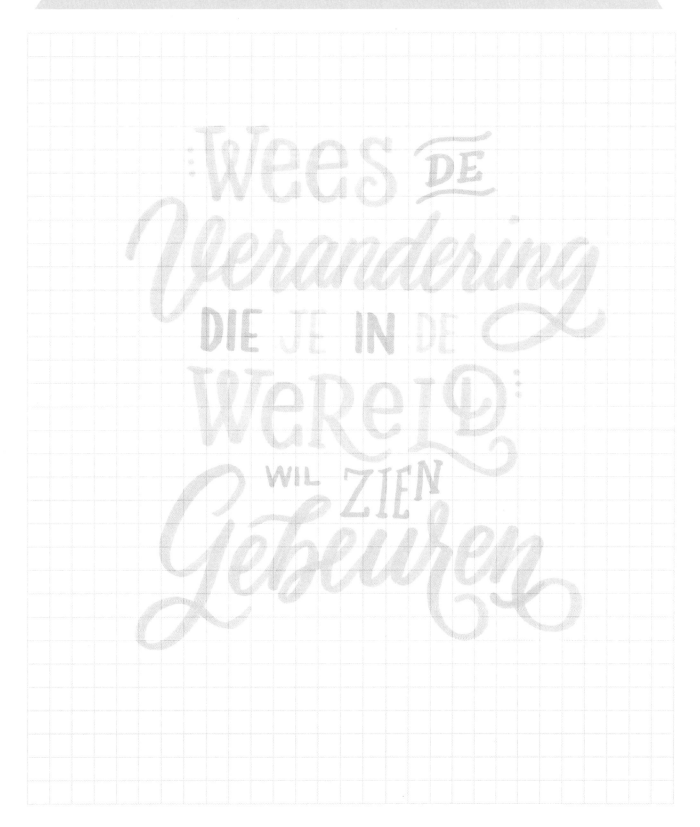

Place tracing paper over sheet or remove and photocopy

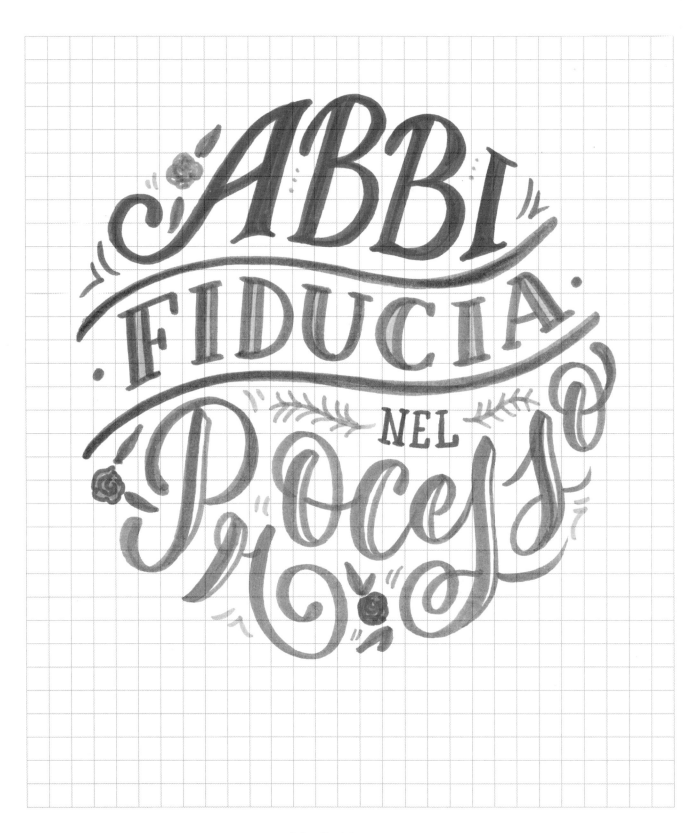

Italian: Trust the process

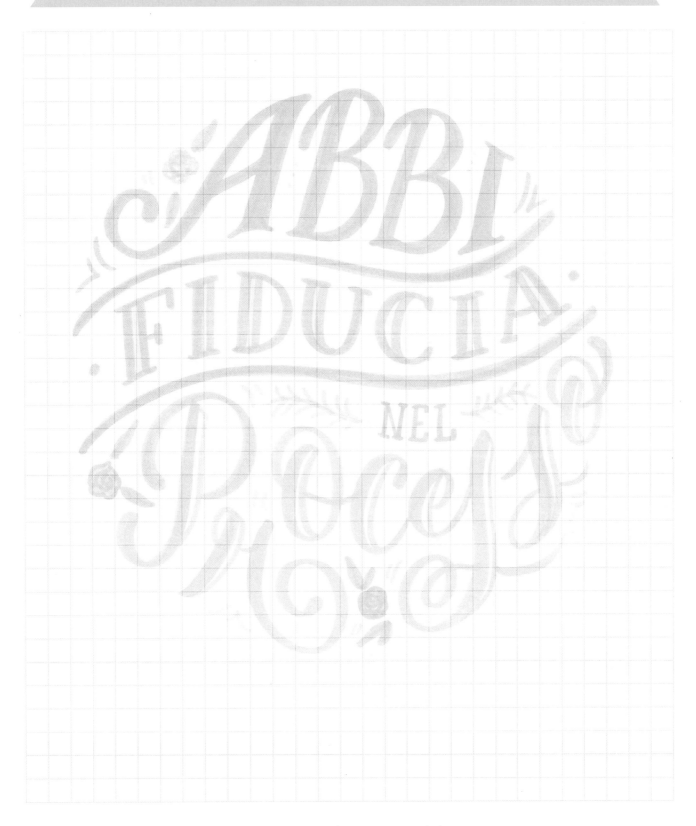

Place tracing paper over sheet or remove and photocopy

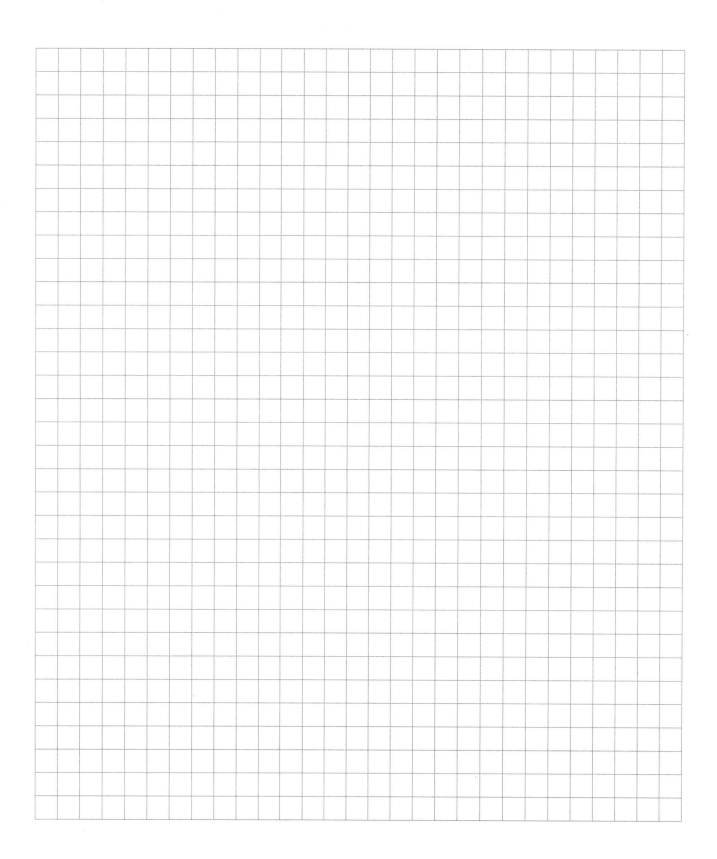

TEMPLATE

Place tracing paper over sheet or remove and photocopy

Acknowledgments

I'd like to give my thanks to the following for helping make this workbook possible:

Judith Cressy, for entrusting me to write *Hand Lettering A to Z*, my first international title (which led to creating this workbook);

Joy Aquilino, my editor, for being supportive and helpful in putting out ideas for this workbook—as well as making sure everything went according to plan;

Marissa Giambrone, my art director, for always keeping tabs on the design aspect of this book and giving me feedback and ideas to improve and learn;

Renae Haines, for overseeing the creation of this workbook;

Rockport Publishers, for publishing this title and making it accessible to everyone around the world;

And to you, for picking up this book. May you find it a useful tool as you go along in your hand lettering journey.

About the Author

Abbey Sy is an artist and author from Manila, Philippines. Best known for her hand-lettering work and travel illustrations, she has worked with a wide range of clients from various industries. She has written and illustrated best-selling books on hand lettering and journaling, including *Hand Lettering A to Z* (Rockport Publishers, 2017), and her art has been recognized on both local and international websites and publications, such as *BuzzFeed*, *DesignTaxi*, and *IdN magazine*, to name a few.

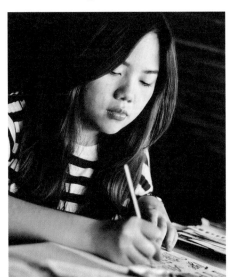

She currently works as a creative entrepreneur—writing and illustrating books, teaching art classes on weekends, and producing her own line of products—in the hopes of further fulfilling her artistic dreams and fueling her passion for both art and travel.

View Abbey's work at
Website: abbey-sy.com
Facebook: fb.com/artbyabbeysy
Twitter & Instagram: @abbeysy

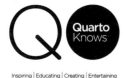

Inspiring | Educating | Creating | Entertaining

Brimming with creative inspiration, how-to projects, and useful information to enrich your everyday life, Quarto Knows is a favorite destination for those pursuing their interests and passions. Visit our site and dig deeper with our books into your area of interest: Quarto Creates, Quarto Cooks, Quarto Homes, Quarto Lives, Quarto Drives, Quarto Explores, Quarto Gifts, or Quarto Kids.

© 2018 Quarto Publishing Group USA Inc.

First published in 2018 by Rockport Publishers, an imprint of The Quarto Group, 100 Cummings Center, Suite 265-D, Beverly, MA 01915, USA.
T (978) 282-9590 F (978) 283-2742 QuartoKnows.com

All rights reserved. No part of this book may be reproduced in any form without written permission of the copyright owners. All images in this book have been reproduced with the knowledge and prior consent of the artists concerned, and no responsibility is accepted by producer, publisher, or printer for any infringement of copyright or otherwise, arising from the contents of this publication. Every effort has been made to ensure that credits accurately comply with information supplied. We apologize for any inaccuracies that may have occurred and will resolve inaccurate or missing information in a subsequent reprinting of the book.

Rockport Publishers titles are also available at discount for retail, wholesale, promotional, and bulk purchase. For details, contact the Special Sales Manager by email at specialsales@quarto.com or by mail at The Quarto Group, Attn: Special Sales Manager, 100 Cummings Center, Suite 265-D, Beverly, MA 01915, USA.

10 9 8 7 6 5 4 3

ISBN: 978-1-63159-627-8

Digital edition published in 2018
eISBN: 978-1-63159-628-5

Library of Congress Cataloging-in-Publication Data is available

Cover Design: Abbey Sy
Illustration: Abbey Sy

Printed in China